THE LOVE THEOREM

CAMILLA ISLEY

Boldwood

First published in 2019. This edition first publishing in Great Britain in 2023 by Boldwood Books Ltd.

Copyright © Camilla Isley, 2019

Cover Design by BNP Design Studio

The moral right of Camilla Isley to be identified as the author of this work has been asserted in accordance with the Copyright, Designs and Patents Act 1988.

Every effort has been made to obtain the necessary permissions with reference to copyright material, both illustrative and quoted. We apologise for any omissions in this respect and will be pleased to make the appropriate acknowledgements in any future edition.

A CIP catalogue record for this book is available from the British Library.

Paperback ISBN 978-1-83751-913-2

Large Print ISBN 978-1-83751-909-5

Hardback ISBN 978-1-83751-908-8

Ebook ISBN 978-1-83751-906-4

Kindle ISBN 978-1-83751-907-1

Audio CD ISBN 978-1-83751-914-9

MP3 CD ISBN 978-1-83751-911-8

Digital audio download ISBN 978-1-83751-905-7

Boldwood Books Ltd
23 Bowerdean Street
London SW6 3TN
www.boldwoodbooks.com

To all my fellow women engineers...

1

LANA

I hear footsteps outside the door and wonder if the clandestine occupation of a hotel broom closet is a crime punishable by law. Even if it were, no jury would have the heart to convict me after the morning I've had.

Mitigating circumstances—a failed lab experiment, finding out I'm surrounded by liars, almost being run down by a car in my mad dash to downtown LA—would make the case for me. What would the police even charge me with, anyway? Excessive sobbing? Undignified self-pitying?

The footsteps near, and I hold my breath. Whether or not I'm convinced of my justified presence in this closet, I'd rather not have to explain myself to a stranger.

But thankfully whoever was out there walks past, none the wiser about me having taken residence in one of the supply storage rooms of the Peninsula Beverly Hills.

I unlock my phone to check if something has changed—*it hasn't*. The proof that my life is in shambles is still there, spelled in colored pixels. My eyes have barely adjusted to the bright light when I lock the screen again, plunging the tiny room back into darkness.

Emotional and physical distress mingle in the shadows, making it hard to discern what's real from what's imaginary.

The sensation that my brain is about to explode from the million thoughts swirling inside it? Probably a mental projection.

The burning in my throat? I'd say fifty-fifty. It could be from all the sobbing or, equally possible, an emotional manifestation.

The sharp edge of the rack behind me boring holes into my shoulder blades? One hundred percent real. And the only symptom I could fix.

When I can no longer stand the discomfort, I shuffle toward the rear of the room, opting to lean against the back wall in a less thorny position. Also, my butt is hurting from sitting so long on the hard floor. I finger the shelves in the dark, until I come in contact with fluffy towels and stash a couple underneath me.

That's also when I realize I'm impossibly hot. The air conditioning of the hotel doesn't extend to its closets apparently. I lean away from the rack and remove the blue lab coat I hadn't realized I was still wearing. How did I even keep it on until now? The adrenaline must've been cooling me. Ha! Maybe I should introduce it as a new bio-coolant in my research. Nah, hormones and rockets don't mix.

As I sit in near total obscurity, the only light coming from the sliver of space underneath the door, I contemplate all the wrong life choices that brought me to this moment.

There was that time as a two-year-old when I thought it'd be a good idea to befriend the neighborhood's twin kids. That decision at least half backfired on me as one of the twins just stabbed me in the back.

Then there was school and my natural predisposition for scientific subjects that led me to pick aerospace engineering as my major in college. So far, something I'd solidly filed in the pros column of my qualities. Now, I'm reconsidering. A philosopher would be better equipped to deal with the situation and take it, well, *with philosophy*. Or at least use the experience as a case study for deranged humanity and the loss of common social values like friendship, loyalty, basic decency...

But I'm digressing. The gold medal of poor life decision has to go to that day in freshman year when I assumed it'd be harmless to sit next to the hot, dark-eyed nerd in a Statics and Strength of Materials lecture. He was lounging in the first row of the auditorium, acting as if he owned the place. That should've been a red flag for selfish, egocentric tendencies.

In my defense, attractive, non-socially awkward engineers are a rare breed. Most of my fellow freshmen fit best into the *nerdy* nerd category. Skinny, thick-glassed introverts who are more at ease solving partial differential equations than talking to women —not that I'm famously an extrovert.

Even so, is it really my fault that I sat next to the tall guy with broad shoulders, cute dimples, and dashing smile who also gave the impression of being a decent conversationalist?

I'd rather call it a series of unfortunate events that started in year two of my life and culminated in year twenty-eight with a neurotic meltdown in a broom closet.

But, hey, the greatest fantasy saga of all time started with the protagonist living in a broom cupboard. I've only been here an hour. What if this is the beginning of my story?

Yeah, right. Not going to happen. I read too much fiction. Not how real life works.

No matter the angle I consider the situation from, I can't put a positive spin on it.

The sting of the betrayal resurfaces, and fresh tears spring down my cheeks.

Before I can get the waterworks under control, outside noises distract me once again from my misery. Someone is thundering down the hall in a hurry.

I relax. No one could be that hard-pressed to reach cleaning supplies.

The moment I dismiss the threat, the pounding footsteps stop abruptly outside my hidey-hole.

The handle rattles and my heart jumps into my throat. Then the door opens in a flash of blinding light that prevents me from seeing who the invader is before they close the door behind them just as quickly.

That's weird. Am I now confined in a broom closet with a serial killer? Who else would shut themselves in a storage room without turning on the lights? Except for me, of course.

Would anyone hear me if I screamed? Maybe, but then again, what would I say to my rescuers? Help, someone broke into the closet that I have no right to occupy?

"Is someone in here?" a deep male voice asks in a sexy British accent, cutting through my thoughts.

Do serial killers have sexy accents?

2

CHRISTIAN

I race down the service hall until I find a door with a "personnel only" sign. I try the handle; it turns. In a flash, I rush in and shut the closet door behind me.

Without the outside light, the small room stands in complete darkness, but as I entered, I thought I saw someone sitting on the floor, or... was it just my imagination?

"Is someone in here?" I ask, unsure.

"Who's there?" a shaky female voice replies.

"Sorry to intrude," I say. "I need a place to hide."

"Well, this closet is taken," she wails. "Go away."

"Are you crying?"

"Nooo." Her reply comes out in a howl.

Clearly, the woman *is* crying.

"Should I turn on the lights?"

I grope the wall for a switch, find one, and flip it. But I only get a quick flash of metal racks filled with linens and toiletries before I'm hit over the head by something white and fluffy—a towel.

"Put that along the threshold and keep your voice down," my

fellow stowaway orders. "People outside might notice the light or hear you. You'll get us caught."

I do as she says and then turn around to assess the situation. The hideaway is minuscule and cramped. Two silver racks crammed with supplies are pushed against the walls with only a narrow space in the middle. Exactly what one would expect from a hotel storage room.

The woman sharing this impromptu refuge with me is a young brunette in a white T-shirt with *Science Matters* written across the chest and jeans. She's sitting cross-legged in the sliver of space between the racks, her shoulders leaning against the back wall, a crumpled blue mass of fabric at her side tossed over a messenger bag. Hands in her lap, she's clinging to a phone, its screen dark.

I sit on the opposite side of the closet, resting with my back against the door with a sigh. *I'm knackered.* I fold my legs close to my chest so as not to invade her space too much—even like this our knees are not three feet apart—and study her. She isn't looking at me; she's too busy blowing her nose and wiping tears from her face. But even with a runny nose, red-blotted skin, and tear-streaked cheeks, I can tell she's pretty.

When the lady finally lifts her eyes to meet mine, their color is breathtaking. A deep, vibrant blue that reminds me of the Pacific Ocean on a sunny day. I wait for those two sapphires to widen in recognition as she takes me in, but nothing happens. Not a blink. She barely spares me a glance, then goes back to blowing her nose.

Could she really not have recognized me? Must still be too shocked a random bloke barged in on her hiding place. I wonder what a crying woman is doing stashed away in the broom closet of the Peninsula.

"Hey, are you okay?" I ask.

"Do I look okay to you?" she fires back.

Yeah, Christian, kind of a stupid question.

"I meant, what happened? Why are you hiding in here?"

"Why are you?" she retorts.

Should I tell her I'm running from the paparazzi? No real reason why, but a gut feeling is telling me not to. So I decide not to mention the paps.

"Fair enough," I say. "Want to swap stories?" I tilt my head at her in a silent question.

She nods, so I go ahead and give her an edited version of the truth. This is how, "I met privately with Ridley Scott to discuss his next movie, but the paps busted us as we were leaving," becomes, "I had a meeting about a project I'd like to keep under wraps, but a bunch of people I've worked with in the past appeared in the lobby. Small world, huh?" I try to be casual. "And I couldn't have them see me here today. Hence the closet."

"Secret meeting?" She frowns. "Sounds shady."

I smile. "More confidential, really. What about you?"

"I... I..." She starts the phrase multiple times before collapsing into another fit of sobs. "I'm s-sorry..."

"No, it's okay... err... What's your name?"

"Lana," she says, blows her nose, then looks at me expectantly. "And you?"

Unbelievable. She really has no idea who I am. Not to sound arrogant or anything, but I haven't had to introduce myself to anyone in, well, forever.

"Christian," I say. "Christian Slade."

No reaction. Zero recognition in her eyes. Well, that's new and 100 percent unexpected. Anonymity doesn't happen to me—*ever*. People know who I am. Everyone does, especially women. My face has been on the front page of practically every tabloid, magazine, and online publication in the world. The city is plastered with posters of me, I'm on the side of buses, on billboards, and on digital screens... and, yet, this woman has no clue who she's talking to.

"Hi, Christian." Lana cracks a small smile and, wow, her entire face transforms. "Sorry for breaking down on you. Not my best day."

She reaches into her bag for a stainless-steel bottle and takes a small sip.

"You want some water?" she offers.

"No, thanks. I'm good."

I'm not thirsty, but I'm dying to know what's going on with this woman. Still, it doesn't feel right to pressure her to share. The last thing she needs right now is a nosy stranger. So I watch Lana as she drinks, unlocks the phone in her lap, and stares at the screen for an eternity without uttering a single word. When the display goes dark on its own, a fresh flood of tears rolls down her cheeks.

"Can I do anything for you?"

She sniffles. "Could you check if there are tissues somewhere in here?" She shows me the crumpled white paper in her hands. "This was my last one."

I get up, search the shelves for a box of Kleenex, and hand it to her.

"Thanks." Lana lets out a bittersweet chuckle. "At least I won't run out of tissues." She noisily blows her nose again.

"Are you planning on staying here long?"

"I'm not leaving until they do." She points a finger at the dark screen in her lap.

"Who's they?"

"My boyfriend and my best friend," she says.

Bloody hell.

"Or," she continues, "more like my ex-boyfriend and my ex-best friend."

"Are they... mmm?" How do I ask tactfully? *Impossible.* "Sorry, I don't want to meddle if you're not comfortable talking."

She shrugs. "Talking is better than crying, and at least you're a total stranger. It's not like you can judge me."

"I wouldn't," I say, and relax against the door. "Shoot."

"You have an iPhone?"

Weird question, but I answer anyway. "Yeah?"

"Ever used the Find My app?"

"No. How does it work?"

"It allows you to share your location with your contacts, and for you to see each other's whereabouts at all times."

That sounds like my very own personal hell. Imagine everyone being able to geo-target me at any moment. Oh, the paparazzi would love to have me pinned down like that.

"But you can turn it off, right?" I ask.

"Yeah. To access their location, a contact has to approve you."

"And your boyfriend approved you?"

Seems like a stupid move for someone having an affair.

"Yeah, they both did."

Even more stupid.

"But it was ages ago. I'm talking five or six years ago."

I low-whistle. "Long relationship."

Especially considering I've never made it past the one-year mark.

Lana winces. "Longer, unfortunately; we met in college."

"So, the app?" I prompt.

"Yeah, sorry. We all followed each other on a weekend we went hiking in Big Bear, in case someone got lost. And I guess neither of them thought of withdrawing the approval."

"And the app is telling you they're both here?"

Lana swallows and nods.

"Could they not... I mean, could it be innocent?"

"Two adults booking a room at the Peninsula? They're not here to play Scrabble," she hisses.

No, probably not.

"I'm sorry," I offer. "First time this happened?"

"No, I-I don't think so." Lana takes a deep breath, possibly to stop more tears from coming. "I like to check Johnathan's location from time to time..."

"I'm guessing Johnathan's your boyfriend."

"Yeah. And I'm not a psycho-stalker who likes to track her boyfriend's every move or anything. It was more to see when he was coming home from work so I could set the table or other silly things like that. Always knowing where he was felt... I don't know... comforting?"

Definitely sounds more stalkerish, but better not to contradict an angry, crying woman.

"Anyway," Lana continues. "About two months ago, I saw them in the same location, downtown, at lunchtime. But then afterward, Summer—my best friend—called me and told me she'd bumped into Johnathan and that they'd eaten together, so I didn't read much into it. Not until it happened again last week."

"For the first time in two months?"

"I don't know. It's not like I check the app every day; it's a random thing I do from time to time. When I'm thinking about Johnathan for whatever reason, I have a peek at where he is..."

"So, last week they were together again."

"Mm-hm, lunchtime again, but in Santa Monica this time, which is as far as it gets from both their offices."

I shift positions; the floor is hard and uncomfortable to sit on. "And I guess there was no call from Summer this time?"

"No, exactly." Lana pulls her hair away from her cheeks and up into a messy bun. Tendrils trail down, framing her face. She's cute.

"And when I texted Summer to ask how she was doing, she told me she'd been stuck in the office all day."

"A lie."

"Yeah. That night I asked Johnathan about *his* day and he, too, lied. Said he had a business meeting in Malibu. No mention of a pit stop in Santa Monica. As you said, I tried to come up with an alternative, logical, innocent explanation. The app isn't super precise. They could've been in the same neighborhood without being together. But even so, why lie?"

"Only one reason I can think of."

"Right." Lana stares back down at her phone, unlocks the screen, grimaces, and locks it. "After that day, I turned into a real stalker. I've been obsessed with the app ever since. And today, *bingo*, I caught them in the same place again. So I hopped on the first bus and followed them here."

"And you're sure they're in the hotel?"

"Both their cars are in the parking lot."

"They could've gone somewhere else."

"I called reception and asked to speak to Johnathan. They connected me to his room." Lana grimaces. "He didn't even bother with a fake name. Anyway, I pretended to be the concierge checking in to see if everything was okay. I could hear Summer's voice in the background, asking who was on the phone. They're here together, probably having sex right as we speak, and... oh... oh, gosh..." Lana starts hyperventilating. "There's no air in here..."

She needs something to breathe into. I only find sanitary paper bags on the racks, which isn't the best, but... she's having a panic attack. They'll have to do.

"Here." I open one and give it to her. "Put this over your mouth."

Lana follows my instructions and, after a few deep inhales, she starts to calm down. Or, at least, she stops hyperventilating, which I'm taking as a good sign.

"Sorry," she apologizes.

"Don't be. I don't know what I'd do if our roles were reversed."

Probably would've already knocked the damn room door down and started throwing punches. At least her way doesn't end in an assault charge.

"Can we... Can we talk about something else?" Lana asks.

"Like what?"

"Tell me about you. What do you do? What's the secret project about?"

Ah, a direct question. I could skid the truth again, but no, I don't want to lie to Lana. She's already had enough fibs fed to her.

"I'm an actor," I say. "I'm working on a new movie."

Her mouth curls into a little smile.

"What?" I ask, self-consciously.

"You're just so LA." Her smile widens. "Is this an actual movie we're talking about, or are you really a bartender walking around with headshots in your pockets, hoping to be discovered?"

Maybe fifteen years ago.

"No, I've done some work already." That's, like, the understatement of the century. I've featured in so many box office hits, and I've been the top-grossing actor in Hollywood for almost a decade. "You might've seen me?"

"No, sorry," she says. "I don't watch TV."

No kidding!

"You don't go to the movies?" I ask.

"Nope. I prefer to read books or spend time outdoors..."

As she talks, Lana almost unconsciously unlocks her phone. Only this time, she jolts, sitting up straighter.

"They're on the move!" Her eyes track the screen for a few

seconds. "They're both heading back to their offices. Guess they finished their business and now it's life as usual."

"What are you going to do?"

"Take the bus home and pack Johnathan's stuff before he comes back tonight," Lana says determinedly. "I want that bastard out of our house."

"Hey, you want a ride?" I ask on impulse. "I came here in my car."

"No, thanks. I don't drive by choice. There's enough pollution around already. Californian weather is nice enough to walk anywhere I need to go, and if it's too far, I use public transportation."

"Oh, but I drive electric."

The lie escapes my lips before I know what I'm saying. My Ferrari California may be a sweet ride, but it's not exactly eco-friendly.

"Traffic is terrible at this hour," she protests.

"Traffic is terrible at any hour in LA," I counter. "I promise, it's no trouble at all."

Why am I so hell-bent on giving this woman a ride home? I don't know her. Her problems aren't mine. But I'm not heartless, and it doesn't seem fair to make her battle public transportation on top of everything else.

"You don't even know where I live."

"Where do you live?"

"Westwood."

"Perfect, it's on the way..." ...*opposite to my house*, I finish silently. But I don't care if I have to cross the city twice over and get stuck in rush-hour traffic; I still want to give her a ride.

As the indecision shows on her features, I hold my breath. Is she going to accept my offer?

3

LANA

I stare at the gorgeous, probably non-serial killer stranger offering me a ride home, studying his features in an attempt to determine if I can trust him or not.

The friendly, charming smile, electric green-blue eyes, disheveled blond waves, and heart rate-flattening dimple say "yes". I don't see any red flags. Normal clothes—if not a little showy of his muscled arms and chest. Easy vibe. No visible cartel tattoos declaring his affiliation to a criminal enterprise, or scars tracing a possibly violent past, or icky cologne. Not that poor taste in perfume would warrant discrimination against a person's character. But it's not bad that he has a pleasant scent with cedar and vetiver notes that feels sexy without being overpowering.

The temptation to accept is strong. But so is the doubt. I've already shown a pattern of not making the best decisions, so I'm not sure getting in a car with the tall, blond, dimpled stranger is the best idea.

I try to make a list of pros and cons in my head.

Pros:

It was already seventy-five degrees outside when I rushed

downtown at noon, and now it's 2 p.m., it's probably even hotter. The idea of having to drag my feet back out over the scorching concrete, carrying a bag laden with textbooks I didn't have time to drop off at the Science and Engineering Library in my hurry to get here, and then ride home in a bus packed with sweaty strangers is daunting.

Besides avoiding the potentially upsetting body odors of a packed bus ride, if I go with him, I'll be home sooner. Which will give me more time to pack Johnathan's stuff before that double-crosser, sorry excuse for a man, gets home.

Also, Christian is cute. Smells good. And in the forty-five minutes we've been sharing this closet, he hasn't been anything other than respectful, both physically and mentally. He's let me explain things at my own pace, without badgering me with questions or pressing me to talk about things I'm not ready to discuss while keeping rigorously to his side of the closet.

Still, it could all be a ruse to lure me into his car, and then murder me in an abandoned canyon somewhere.

This brings me to the cons:

I don't know this guy at all.

Riding in a car with a stranger is never a good idea—at least according to every cautionary tale out there.

He is almost *too* attractive. It's not unusual for aspiring actors to be dramatic with their appearance—including sexing it up with the way they dress. But I've been fooled by good looks before. Bad boys often come in handsome packages.

And while he's been cool, calm, and collected thus far, I have no idea what his mental state is outside of this closet.

Isn't hiding in a closet a red flag enough? I know, I'm the pot calling the kettle black, but still.

"I don't know you," I say, feeling better reasoning aloud.

"That's a fair point," he says, shifting slightly.

He must be as uncomfortable as I am sitting on the floor. I throw him another towel.

"Oi," he protests as it misses his face by a couple of inches. "What was that for?"

"To put under your butt."

"Thank, I guess." He re-folds the towel, thickening the cushion effect and sits on it. "Much better."

I wave him off. "Don't mention it. Listen," I go back to the previous topic. "Normally, I'm not someone who'd get into a car with a stranger."

He raises his hands. "I promise I have no bad intentions."

"Which is what any savvy serial killer would say."

He flashes me that dimpled grin and my heart skips a beat.

Christian laughs, lowering his hands. "Okay, fair point. How about this? You can ask me as many questions as you want. If you still don't trust me after that, we go our separate ways."

"You could lie with every answer."

"True." He shrugs. "Then I guess you'll just have to go with your gut. What is your instinct telling you? Am I to be trusted?"

He tilts his head, knitting his brows in a cute half-frown that makes my stomach do twirly flippy things.

I can't help but smile. It's funny how appealing honesty can be. "Let's say I trust you won't try to kill me on the way home."

"That's a start," he says with a wink. "Is it a yes to the ride, then?"

4

CHRISTIAN

"Yes." Lana sags back against the wall. "Thank you for braving LA traffic for me."

"It's no problem," I say, waving my hand dismissively. "All part of the service."

Lana grins at me, and a weird flutter flits over my heart at knowing I made her smile. That she isn't crying anymore partially because of me.

I must be staring too intensely because she shifts uncomfortably. "Are you good to go, or are the people you're hiding from still out there?"

I look away to let up on her unease and fish my phone out of my pocket. "Let me check real quick."

That's when the other shoe drops. I'm screwed. She's never going to believe the Ferrari is electric.

I think of the car's thundering roar... *No chance.*

Unless.

I text my assistant, Penny; she's my only hope.

TO PENNY

I need you to buy me a Tesla

Bring it by the Peninsula parking lot in Beverly Hills

Swap it with the Ferrari

Leave the keys under the front tire

Her reply arrives two seconds later.

FROM PENNY

Should I even ask?

TO PENNY

No

FROM PENNY

How long do I have?

Kudos to Penny for understanding right away that time is of the essence.

TO PENNY

Half an hour tops

FROM PENNY

On it, Boss

I can always count on her. Penelope Jones is the most efficient PA on the planet.

FROM PENNY

But you should give me a raise

And the cockiest.

TO PENNY

Tell you what

Get me a Tesla in 30 min

And you can keep the Ferrari for the day and go shopping with my credit card

FROM PENNY

Those are dangerous words

Never give your credit card to a woman

TO PENNY

You're no ordinary woman

I know I can trust you

She replies with a smiling devil emoji.

"Everything all right?" Lana asks.

I stare up from the phone at her. "Would you mind waiting a little longer? To make sure everyone downstairs is gone."

"No problem."

We fall into silence, which quickly becomes awkward.

"What about you?" I eventually ask. "You haven't told me what you do."

"I'm a Ph.D. student at UCLA."

I smirk. "From the T-shirt, I guess you're not researching ancient history?"

"No, I'm writing my dissertation on thermochemical imaging for the reaction layer in hybrid rockets. I'm trying to use laser absorption tomography to improve the design of the motor and the combustion performance."

"Sorry, you lost me at thermochemical."

"I'm an aerospace engineer researching hybrid rocket propulsion and doubling as a TA."

"Wow. A rocket scientist, huh? I wouldn't have guessed—"

"Yeah, I get that a lot," she interrupts me, suddenly on the defensive. "Not many women in my line of work. But we're trying to change that."

"We?"

"I volunteer as a tutor at charter schools, and I try to steer as many girls as I can toward scientific subjects, to empower them."

A tutor, huh? Wouldn't it be a weird coincidence if she worked at one of my schools?

"Really? I donate to a similar charity..." I say. *More like I'm the founder.* "Teachers Without Postcodes—ever heard of it?"

"Yeah, that's the charity that sponsors my charter school."

Call it destiny?

"Oh, which neighborhood?" I ask.

"Compton. The kids there are so smart..."

Once I've gotten her onto a subject she's clearly passionate about, the conversation flows. Thirty minutes later, we're enthusiastically discussing the need for a fairer education system when my phone pings.

FROM PENNY

Swap made

Keys under the front tire

TO PENNY

Cheers

FROM PENNY

You're so British sometimes O.o

Anyway, have fun with the Tesla

I sure will with the Ferrari

As I read Penny's text, I grin and shake my head.

"Everything all right?" Lana asks.

"Yeah, my unwanted guests should've cleared out by now. Ready to go?"

"Sure, perfect."

I get up and offer my hand to pull her up. When our eyes become level, a breath catches in my lungs.

Man, what kind of trouble are you getting yourself into?

* * *

To avoid getting recognized by anyone, I guide Lana through the service halls until we enter the underground parking lot. I've come and gone this way enough times over the years to navigate the corridors of the Peninsula without trouble.

In the garage, I head to the spot where I'd parked the Ferrari and eye my new ride. Penny bought me a red Tesla; not quite the Ferrari-red I'm used to, but still a nice color.

I stride to the driver's side of the car and make a show of dropping my keys. This gives me the perfect excuse to bend down and collect the new ones my PA has hidden. Only, instead of a regular key, I find a key card on the ground that looks more suited to opening a hotel room than a car. It has the Tesla logo on it, though, so this must be what I need.

"Wow." Lana has come around to stand beside me. "This looks brand new."

You have no idea.

"Yeah, I just got it."

"Cool." She walks around the car to the passenger door and waits for me to unlock it. Despite her laidback comment, her eyes dart around the empty garage and her smile wavers. I'd better hurry before she decides she's better off with public transportation.

With the key card in my hand, I feel like a total moron. I have no clue how to get this car to open. Where's the card reader? Is that even a thing with cars?

Placing the card next to the door handle doesn't work. With beads of sweat blossoming on my forehead, I search for other possible places to stick this key.

Where would they put the opening mechanism?

The shell of the car looks the same all over, except for a lighter patch of glass between the two side windows. For lack of better alternatives, I press the card to the doorframe and wait for something to happen. When the Tesla finally beeps and unlocks, I sigh with relief and get in.

Two seconds later, I'm in a panic again. There's no start button near the wheel, or any other button or key slot, only a giant screen sitting in the middle of the dashboard.

How do I turn this thing on?

Pretending I have to check a message on my phone, I quickly pull up a user manual on the internet. The instructions say I have to place the key card near the cup holder and push the brake to start the engine.

Engine successfully started, I pull my seat belt on and ask Lana for her address.

She gives it to me, and I try to work the screen to input our destination. The map is already there; how hard can it be? But after a few unlucky touches, I only manage to turn on the radio super loud, turn it off, and make the car tell me off with two angry beeps.

"Sorry," I say to Lana, trying not to look too frazzled. "Car's new; I still have to get used to all this"—I gesture at the screen—"technology."

"No problem." She smiles. "I can give you directions the old-fashioned way."

"Great, thanks. Can you pass me the hat in the glove compartment?"

Whenever I drive, I always wear a baseball cap. Saves me from being recognized by the paparazzi, or anyone else, really. Penny knows. And I'm sure she left me one.

Lana opens the compartment and hands me a black-and-white cap with a green peace sign printed in the middle. I'm unable to suppress a smirk as I put it on. Penny must have been cackling to herself as she picked it out; a literal Greenpeace hat. The woman knows how to be sarcastic.

As I merge into traffic, Lana directs me onto Wilshire Boulevard. From there, it's basically a straight ride all the way to Westwood.

"My home is the one with the blue door," Lana informs me twenty minutes later.

I pull up in front of a two-story townhouse, the bottom half white, and the upper floor painted a light blue. I kill the engine and stare at Lana, at a loss for words. What do you say to someone who just had her life ripped apart by the two people she trusted the most in the world?

"Thanks for the ride," Lana says.

"It was nothing."

She bites her lower lip but makes no move to get out of the car.

"Is something the matter?" I ask.

"Sorry." She hides her face in her hands. "It's... I'm not sure if I'm ready to go in there alone."

"You want me to come with you?"

"No, no. Thank you." She looks up at me with big, scared blue eyes. "I've already abused your kindness too much."

"Actually..." I massage my throat. "I'm parched. You wouldn't happen to have some of that water left?"

She doesn't; I saw her finish the bottle while we were in the closet.

I've given her the perfect excuse to invite me in, and her lips curl as her eyes go bright. It's like a secret, inside-joke smile.

"My bottle is empty, but I have drinks inside," she says. "Would you like to come in?"

"Sure." I put the key card in my jeans pocket and we both get out of the car.

As we enter the house, the bohemian-hippy clashing colors of the interior almost make my eyes water. The furniture is intentionally-scratched wood, colored textiles, and the odd bronze decoration. At first glance, Lana's house appears messy, but after a closer look, I realize that it's just filled to the brim with books, pillows, rugs, and little tables and cabinets that occupy every available corner.

Rather the opposite of my pristinely white, minimalist Trousdale Estates crib.

"Wow, lots of colors here," I say.

"I know." Lana shuts the door. "I can't stand those soulless houses with all white surfaces and stainless-steel appliances." *And she's basically described my house.* "I need to surround myself with furniture that has character."

I take off the Greenpeace hat and follow her into the living room, where she points me to the pink-blue-orange-green couch. "Please sit here. Is water fine, or do you prefer something else? Iced tea? Pineapple juice?"

"Iced tea would be great, thanks."

As I sit and wait for her to come back, I notice there's no TV in the living room. When she said she doesn't watch television, I assumed it meant she just didn't turn it on much, not that she doesn't even have one. Hence her having no inkling of who I am.

I haven't been able to talk to someone who wasn't biased by my job and fame for I can't remember how long... Over a decade for sure.

Is this why I feel an inexplicable pull toward Lana? Is it the novelty of her seeing me as a regular person?

Two abnormally fat cats jump onto the couch, interrupting my musings. The tabby kitties look like twins, both with lush, light-brown fur and big yellow eyes.

"Hello," I say.

One cat walks over my legs to go perch on the left armrest, while his doppelganger sits on my other side. I tentatively scratch the cat to my right, my hand disappearing within his long fur. Maybe they're not fat; they just have loads of hair.

The kitty seems to appreciate the attention because, after a while, he curls up against my thigh and goes to sleep. The other one is still seated and looking at me expectantly. I give him a scratch, too, and when he's contented, he settles on the armrest.

"Oh, I see you've made friends." Lana is back with my glass of iced tea. "Did they molest you?"

"Just demanded a scratch," I say, then thank her as she hands me the glass and sits on a blue knitted pouf next to the couch. "You've had them for long?"

"Adopted them two years ago, but they're a little older. Since they weren't kittens, nobody wanted them, so I took them in. They're brothers."

"Yeah, I could tell. Do they have names?"

"Cengel and Boles," she says.

"Wow, they sound like important names."

Here comes the inside-joke smile again.

"Should I recognize the names from somewhere?" I ask.

The smile widens. "Only if you were a nerd and an engineer. Dr. Yunus A. Cengel and Michael A. Boles are the co-authors of the most widely adopted thermodynamics manual all mechanical and aerospace engineering students have to face at one point. We all call the book 'Cengel and Boles' for short."

I don't have the faintest idea what a thermodynamics manual might contain, and for a second there, I'm overwhelmed by how smart this woman must be to be an aerospace engineer.

I never failed a class in high school, but I'm no genius. My scientific savviness stops at what I was forced to learn in sixth form. My acting career took over before I could finish university. Not much of a scholar here.

"We thought it was funny." Lana shrugs, and the smile disappears from her lips.

"Is your boyfriend an engineer, too?"

"Yeah, we fell for each other freshman year, had most courses together. But he works for an aerospace company now. Academia has never been his thing."

"Still planning on packing all his stuff before he comes home tonight?"

Lana lowers her gaze for a second, then trains those deep blue eyes on me with a new resolution sparkling in them. "Yeah, and I should start if I want to be done before he gets here."

She stands up as if, decision made, she wants to get down to business right away. I sense it's also my cue to go; she needs to do this alone. So I finish my tea in one long sip and get up as well. "I'll leave you to it."

We walk to the door and I step outside, awkwardly hovering on her doorstep. "I guess this is goodbye, then."

She nods. "Thanks again for the ride." Then she bites her full lower lip in a way I'm sure she doesn't know could make a man lose his mind, and adds, "Wait here a second."

Lana disappears inside the house and comes back a minute later holding a business card. She hands it to me, and I read her full name: Lana Voynich. I turn the card and notice with a thrill she has handwritten her phone number on the back.

When I raise my gaze again, she's blushing and blabbing, "If you ever need an aerospace consultancy..."

"You'll be the first one I call." I smile, and before I know what I'm doing, I pull her into a hug and whisper, "Good luck with everything."

We pull apart, facing each other even more awkwardly than before, and she nods. "Thank you, I'll need it."

"Gotta go now." I put the Greenpeace cap back on and hop the few steps down the curb to my brand new Tesla.

Still not used to the key card or the driving system, I pull away from Lana's house in understated silence. The rumbling engine of the Ferrari would've made for a much more dramatic exit.

5

LANA

I shouldn't have given him my number.

Call me if you ever need an aerospace consultancy.

So lame. What was I thinking?

You were pissed and feeling a little vindictive toward your jackass of a boyfriend, so you gave the cute guy your number.

Cute. The guy isn't *cute*, he's trouble. Eyes too bright, face too handsome, smile too dashing. Not to talk about the British accent. Right, too much on my plate already.

Ah.

Fury mixes with bitterness as I yank one of Johnathan's shirts off its hanger and curl it into a tight ball. When the fabric is all crumpled, I stuff the shirt into the open suitcase on the bed.

Johnathan likes his work button-downs to be starched, pristine, and crisp. No one hates creases more than he does.

Aha.

Vengeful delight fills me as I grab the last dry-cleaned shirt and cram it messily next to the others in the case.

Never had more fun packing! Right! Tears threaten to start spilling again, but I fight them back and focus on taking out my rage on Johnathan's clothes.

Cengel must sense something is wrong because he appears in the bedroom and jumps on the bed with a long meow.

"No, darling, Mom's not okay."

He bumps his head against my thigh and I scratch him behind the ears. But feline empathy only goes so far. Cengel soon loses interest in me and eyes the open suitcase with keenness.

If there's something Johnathan hates more than wrinkled clothes, it's clothes coated in cat hair. We used to have countless arguments about keeping the cats out of the bedroom—and the bedroom closet in particular. Especially when we were packing for a trip and unattended, open suitcases were left lying around. Apparently, luggage, like boxes, is a premium napping location for kitties, even more so once they sensed case-sleeping was a big no-no for their humans.

"Go ahead, then," I tell Cengel.

He eyes me surreptitiously.

"No, it's not too good to be true. Mommy is being serious; you can sleep in the suitcase."

As if to test me, Cengel places both his front paws on the brim of the suitcase. When I don't protest, he dives in, kneads Johnathan's clothes, purring loudly, and finally settles down.

His twin, probably sensing a great injustice is taking place, hops on the bed only a few minutes later. He throws his brother a dirty look and then stares up at me accusingly.

"You can sleep in the case, too," I reassure Boles. "Let me pad the other side for you."

I snatch a row of Johnathan's carefully folded sweaters out of a drawer, crumple them a little, and lay them at the bottom of the case as bedding.

I pick Boles up and drop him on top. "Here you go."

He seems undecided at first, his feline nature probably telling him that if his human wants him to sleep somewhere, then he shouldn't. But suitcase naps are too inviting to pass up, so in the end, he curls up next to his brother.

I sit on the bed and watch the two of them doze, a bittersweet smile on my face at the tufts of hair already dusting Johnathan's clothes. I scratch Boles behind the ears, and his loud purring gives me the strength to finish packing the bedroom.

Once the closet and dresser are taken care of, I move into the bathroom and unceremoniously throw Johnathan's toiletries into a gym duffle bag. By 7 p.m., I've packed all his things and, except for the array of suitcases waiting in the living room, it could be as if Johnathan had never lived here.

The bastard, however, doesn't get home at the usual time. Guess that with the extended lunch break, he had to pull long hours at the office to make up for it. The tracking app is telling me he's still at work.

When his dot finally starts moving, I sit on a stool at the kitchen bar and wait for him, eyes glued to the front door. The more time that passes with no sign of Mr. Cheater, the angrier I get. Emotions run wild in a rollercoaster of betrayal, rage, sadness, anxiety, uncertainty, pain... until the cycle starts anew and I'm back to being angry again.

Not just at Johnathan, but at Summer, too. *Especially* at her. At the thought of my best friend's disloyalty, my anxiety spikes, making my hands shake so hard I have to drop them on the counter to control the tremor. How could she?

My eyes burn from a mixture of frustration and impatience. I can't think about Summer now; I don't want Johnathan to find me crying. I have to save the last scraps of dignity I have left. When I finally hear the key turn in the lock, I've chewed my nails to shreds and I'm exhausted. Still, my heart starts beating super-fast as a fresh rush of adrenaline floods my veins.

I watch Johnathan walk into the house as if it were any other night.

"Hi, honey," he says. "Sorry I'm so late. Had a terrible day at the office."

Whoa, what a performer.

A sneaky, cheating, lying bastard. How can he act so naturally after having spent the afternoon screwing the brains out of my best friend?

How?

"I had a pretty horrible day, too," I say.

A raging understatement.

For a moment, I'm tempted to ask what has made his day so bad and listen as he feeds me more lies. See how far he'll go. But, frankly, I'm drained, and I can't wait for him to be out of the house and out of my life.

"Oh, I'm sorry. What—" He stops mid-sentence as he spots the suitcases. "Are we going somewhere?" He frowns. "Because I'm super busy at work. I can't take any days off."

Don't worry, I think bitterly in my head, *I won't whisk you away from your mistress.*

"Really, Lana," Johnathan says, starting to look annoyed now. "You know I don't like surprises."

"Relax," I snap. "I haven't planned a romantic gateway if that's what you're worried about."

"So what's with the suitcases?"

Again, I've imagined a million possible sarcastic replies in my head. Something like, "Since you already paid for a room at the Peninsula..." But I'm too tired for sarcasm, and I want to end this farce, so I go with the simple truth: "I know about you and Summer."

Johnathan's neck snaps toward me so fast I'm afraid it might break. Our eyes meet, and a wide range of emotions appear on his face: shock, fear, embarrassment... But to my utter dismay, his features settle on relief.

"Shit," he says, scratching the back of his head. "That's not how we wanted you to find out."

Such a simple response, yet it tells me all I need to know. Taking his answer as the hypothesis for my failed relationship theorem, I come to three logical conclusions:

1. Johnathan *wanted* me to find out. (His visibly relieved expression incontrovertible proof.)
2. He's chosen *her*. They're a "we" now, apparently. He won't even try to beg me for forgiveness. (Not that I would ever forgive him.) But a bit of groveling would've at least given me the satisfaction of showing him all my contempt. Also, it would've helped me believe I haven't thrown away the last ten years of my life on a complete douchebag. And this brings me to realization number three:
3. The asshole didn't even say he was sorry!

In fact, Johnathan is more curious than contrite when he asks, "How did you...?"

No point in keeping the suspense alive. "The Find My app. Neither of you removed me from your followers."

He makes a "so-dumb" grimace and seems at a loss for what to say next, so I take over. "I've packed all your stuff. I want you out of the house tonight."

Still wordless, he stares back and forth between me and the suitcases. Then he acknowledges my request with a single nod.

And just like that, a ten-year relationship is over.

It all feels so anti-climactic.

Johnathan silently loads the bags into his car. When he comes back inside, though, he seems to want to talk.

"Listen, Lana—"

"Don't," I interrupt him. Nothing he could say now would make me feel better. No excuses, justifications, not even a simple apology, would change things. Fighting to keep my tone even, I add, "I'll need your keys back before you go."

Johnathan's eyes widen at the hardness in my voice. Looking chastened, he nods and unhooks his keys from the chain to drop them on the small cabinet in the hall. We stare at each other for a long, silent moment until I break.

"Please go," I whisper.

He nods again and, without another word, he leaves.

Once the door closes, I let myself collapse on the kitchen floor to cry. I'm not sure if it's a nervous reaction, if I'm sad, mad, at him, at *her*, I don't know... My feelings are so all over the place right now, I can't sort myself out.

With a stomach knotted too tight to eat anything, I skip dinner. I change into my PJs, lift a cat under each arm, and go to bed. I changed the sheets earlier. Not that our bed has seen much action lately, but I'm sure Johnathan and I had sex at least once or twice in the past two months.

How creepy that he would still sleep with me while he was cheating with someone else.

I shiver in the dark, wondering if he's already told her. If they're together right now, discussing me and everything that happened. On impulse, I open the Find My app and check their locations. Johnathan is at Mike's house, his best friend, and Summer is driving down the 405. I unfollow both of them so I'll no longer be able to torture myself with what they're doing.

Maybe Summer doesn't know yet that the cat is out of the bag.

Will she try to contact me when Johnathan tells her? Apologize?

I've known Summer even longer than Johnathan. We've been friends since we could walk. Me, her, and her identical twin, Winter—I know, parents can have a questionable sense of humor when naming their children—have been a fantastic trio from that first afternoon I chased a ball into the neighbors' yard. Inseparable ever since.

They say twins have a special connection. Well, with Summer and Winter, I've always felt like the third twin. Growing up, we had other friends but none with whom we shared such a close bond. No boyfriend, roommate, or colleague has ever felt to me like family. Summer and Winter do. *Did.* They've always been more like sisters than best friends... or at least, they were... *How could Summer do this? Stab me in the back over a guy? Did Winter know? How deep does the conspiracy go?*

I spend the night tossing and turning with nightmares of Summer and Johnathan together, having sex, mocking me, laughing at my foolishness.

Between the nightmares, I dream of the stranger who gave me a ride home; only Christian is their accomplice, and he's helping them sneak around behind my back...

My mind is so twisted it keeps coming up with horror-like scenarios: Winter telling me she's siding with her sister and that we can no longer be friends. My students making fun of the naïve TA in the middle of a lecture. My adviser refuting my dissertation because if I'm so dumb I didn't even notice my boyfriend and my best friend were having an affair how could I ever prove I'm capable of conducting independent research? Our friends all siding with them... And so on, and so on, until, finally, I languish in a dreamless slumber.

6

LANA

A double ring of the doorbell wakes me up the next morning.

I'm not sure what time it is but, judging from the bright light filtering in through the blinds, it must be late.

Shoot. What time *is it?* I sit straight up in bed; no matter that my life is falling apart, I have so much work to do besides classes and my research that I can't afford even a day spent moping. At least I didn't have any lectures to give this morning.

Why didn't the alarm sound?

I grab my phone and swipe my thumb up, but the screen stays dark. Right, guess I forgot to charge it last night.

The doorbell sounds again. I've no idea who it could possibly be.

Was I expecting a delivery?

No, I don't remember ordering anything online.

Did *Johnathan* have a delivery scheduled?

Yeesh.

How long will I keep receiving his mail?

Will I wake up every day to find a reminder of his betrayal right in my mailbox?

He'd better find a new address where he can forward his corre-spondence.

Oh, gosh, will he move in with Summer?

Has he already?

My stomach churns at the thought. Either that or my internal organs are protesting after a skipped dinner. Anyway, I don't care whose mail they're trying to deliver, or if I can't afford a single day off work if I want to finish my degree in time, I'm not getting up. I'm going to stay in bed nestled between my two cats and lick my wounds in private. If my adviser disagrees, to hell with him too.

I'm snuggling deeper under the sheets when the buzzer goes off again, and again... and again. That seems a little aggressive for the mail guy. Maybe it's an important parcel that needs signing.

"All right!"

I slither out of bed, trying not to disturb their sleeping majesties, and stroll to the entrance hall in my PJs. Rattled by the aggressive buzzing, I fling the door open without checking through the peephole.

When I see the person on the landing, my first instinct is to sucker punch her in the stomach. But then I take in her clothes—flip-flops, khaki cargo Bermuda pants, plain white T-shirt. Her uneven, white-circles-around-the-eyes face tan. And the messy bun—a real, hair-that-hasn't-seen-conditioner-in-a-month tangle of golden locks. And my brain clicks. Summer would never dress so casually. She's not standing on my doorstep, her twin is.

"Hi," I say.

"Whoa." Winter winces. "For a moment there I thought you were going to throttle me."

"Sorry. It's just that—"

"I share a face with the devil," she finishes the sentence for me.

"Oh, so you know."

"Just found out." She steps forward and pulls me into a tight hug. "I'm so sorry."

I wrap my arms around Winter's warm body, relishing the human contact, tears already welling in my eyes.

"Shhhh," she soothes. "It's going to be all right, and I brought donuts."

I pull back, noticing for the first time the pink box she's holding.

Winter flashes me a goofy smile. "Double glaze!"

I manage not to start crying and beckon her to come in. "Want coffee to go with those?"

"Yes, please, the jet lag is killing me!"

We move into the kitchen and I get busy with the coffee machine.

"When did you get back?" I ask.

Winter is a travel photographer and never stays in LA for long.

"Only last night..."

"Where were you this time?"

"Madagascar."

"How was it?"

"Amazing, but do you really want to talk about an island in the middle of the Indian Ocean right now?"

I turn my back to her and grab two mugs. "No, not really," I admit. The machine beeps; I fill the mugs and settle at the bar next to my friend. "So, how did you find out?"

Winter gives her donut a savage bite. "The evil twin came to pick me up at the airport last night," she says with her mouth half full, "and when I walked out of the gate, I found her crying while she was talking on the phone."

"With Johnathan?" I ask. Acid rises in my throat at saying the name, and I temper it with a bite of fried, saturated fats covered in sugar. Just what I needed.

"Yeah." Winter washes down the donut with a generous sip of coffee. "Summer wouldn't tell me anything at first, but then it's not like she could keep the affair a secret, not since they were already busted!"

My chest tightens. It's still hard to process which betrayal is worse: Johnathan's or Summer's. "And then... what did she say?"

"Sure you want to hear the pathetic stream of excuses she came up with...?"

I nod.

"Well, it was the usual. She felt alone and sad after breaking up with Robert... It started innocently at first— she bumped into Johnathan by chance a few times. They clicked, things spiraled out of control..." Winter makes a pretend-gag face. "She made it sound as if you could accidentally sleep with someone."

"Yeah, they just happened to find hotel rooms booked in their name, right?" I say. "An affair that lasts months is no mistake. And what if I hadn't caught them? How long would they have kept at it?"

"Summer claims she fell in love and didn't know how to stop... She hoped Johnathan would break up with you, but also didn't want you to suffer, and a bunch of other trite crap..."

I blanch at this. "In love? Summer said she's *in love*?"

Winter's eyes widen. "Oh, I'm sorry, was I too flat?"

"No," I reassure her. "I need someone to be straight with me. I touched my lowest point yesterday; I can't deal with any more artifice."

Winter squeezes my hand across the counter. "Honey, you have nothing to be ashamed of."

I wince. "Because you don't know I spent yesterday afternoon hidden in a closet at the Peninsula waiting for them to finish having sex while crying my heart out."

Winter's eyes widen. "You were *there*?"

"Yep, but I couldn't muster the courage to go upstairs and confront them mid-act. How pathetic is that?"

"Not at all. If something like that happened to me, I'd cower in a dark corner as well."

Donuts finished, I refill our mugs and we move to the couch. Five seconds later, each of us has a cat in our laps.

Winter scratches Boles under his chin and asks, "So, how heartbroken are you?"

The question startles me. Of all the things I've felt since Johnathan left last night—angry, betrayed, shocked, anxious, sad, tired—somehow heartbroken hasn't made the list.

"How can you tell if you're heartbroken?" I ask.

"Standard symptoms include a heart-ripped-out-of-chest sensation, palpitations, shivers of panic at the idea of never being able to kiss the loved one again…"

"Mmm," I muse. "Nothing like that. I'm more stunned than anything else. Johnathan has been in my life for so long that losing him feels more like having an arm cut off than my heart ripped out."

"Good."

"How's that good?"

"You can survive without a limb, but it's pretty hard to keep going without a heart. And…" She stops, and twirls a loose lock around her finger, looking undecided whether she should continue.

"Come on, out with it," I prompt her.

"I'm trying to find a silver lining," Winter says. "If breaking up with Johnathan isn't giving you the slightest chest pains, perhaps it isn't all bad you broke up. I mean, he and my sister are two cockroaches who deserve to burn in hell forever, but maybe it was about time you took your relationship with Johnathan behind the barn and shot it."

"Why would you say that?"

"You guys... mmm... lately, seemed a bit flat as a couple."

I curl my fingers into Cengel's fur. "Flat how?"

"Not as into each other..."

"Johnathan clearly wasn't into me since he's been screwing my best friend on the side. And how long is lately?"

Winter scrunches her face in an apologetic grimace. "Couple of years?"

"That long? Really?"

"Yep, you guys were like that thirty-year married couple with nothing to say, instead of one that still has to get engaged and tie the knot."

"After ten years together, a relationship can't be as intense as it was in the beginning," I counter.

"Try to be very honest with yourself, Lana. Are you or are you not in love with Johnathan?"

"I'm confused," I say. "He's been such a big part of my life, I don't even know how to function without him."

"That's co-dependence, not love."

"Yes, but we share the same friends, and now we can't all hang out together. From now on it's going to be: who do we invite, Lana or Johnathan and Summer? Our group is split, ruined. I wonder who'll get custody of whom?"

"Johnathan will get Mike and Ingrid, for sure. Mike is his best friend."

"Oh, but I love Ingrid."

"Well, you'll get to keep Martha and Hector."

"Why?"

"You met Hector in grad school and he's basically a male you. Plus, he could never stand Johnathan."

"Why would you say that?"

She shrugs. "He always thought Johnathan wasn't good enough for you."

"Really?"

"Yes. Plus, Hector is a bit of an academia snob. He considers Johnathan a sellout for working a corporate job."

"Yeah, you're probably right on that."

Winter taps her chin with a finger. "Who's left? Ah, yes, Susan. She was your roommate in grad school so it's safe to assume she'll stick with you."

"So, according to that theory, Daria will take Summer's side."

Winter scrunches her face, pondering. "They were roommates on their semester abroad, true. But you and Daria have grown really close since college, and she detests cheaters after what happened with her last two boyfriends. I'd say she's borderline."

"Oh, please, stop." I cover my face with my hands. "See?" I mumble between my fingers. "Exactly my point. There are going to be factions, and people taking sides. It's not just my romantic life that's ruined, but everything else, too. And there's two of them and one of me. In the end, it'll be easier to keep calling them and leave me out, and I'll end up the single loser with no friends."

"Hey, what about me?" Winter protests. "I'm right here, aren't I?"

"Yeah, thanks for coming." I squeeze her knee. "But it's a coincidence you're in LA. You're gone most of the time."

"Fair enough. No other friends or colleagues you can lean on outside of our group?"

"Not really. I meet up with a few of the other TAs for lunch and coffee sometimes, but it's ridiculous how many colleagues in their twenties are already married and with kids. I've no idea how they can balance doctorate research, on top of the TA job, on top of having a family."

"So your life is screwed," Winter concludes.

"Appears so."

"But you're not heartbroken."

I take a moment to reflect before answering. My feelings for Johnathan haven't been wild in a long time. And I'm definitely more scared of the turmoil this breakup will bring into my life than losing Johnathan per se...

"No," I say. "My heart is bruised but intact."

"Good." Winter's face opens up in a bright smile. "Let's focus on the positives for now."

I crack a grin. "Should I tell you about the handsome stranger with the sexy British accent who rescued me from the Peninsula's closet?"

7

CHRISTIAN

The roaring of the Ferrari coming up the driveway wakes me the next morning.

If Penny is here already... *Time to get up, mate!*

I swipe back the sleeping mask covering my eyes, wearing it above my forehead like a pair of sunglasses, get off the bed, and pull on a robe to go down to breakfast.

As I move along the hall toward the stairs, the framed covers of six issues of *People Magazine*'s Sexiest Man Alive feature gaze down at me from their honorary spot on the wall. I know, a bit narcissistic to keep them on display. Still, I stare fondly at the one from my first win after a few years of being stuck in the top ten.

A turning point in my career. The year when producers around Hollywood understood they'd have to shell out the big bucks to have me in their motion pictures. And also when the blown-up fame allowed me to become pickier with screenplays.

Yep, the covers are staying on the wall.

I wink at my pic and hop down the stairs.

In the kitchen, Jeff, my personal chef, greets me with a cheerful, "Good morning, Mr. Slade, what can I get you for breakfast?"

"Morning, Jeff. Plain yogurt and fresh berries, thank you. I still feel a little heavy from dinner. And coffee." I stifle a yawn. "Plenty of coffee."

"That's because you ate at the competition." He means restaurants. Last night I was out with Marvin, my agent, to discuss the Ridley Scott movie. "You know they use way too much butter in those steakhouses."

He's right; my filet mignon was soaked in a buttery sauce. Still delicious, though.

Penny makes her entrance before I can reply.

"Nice ride, boss." She tosses me the Ferrari keys, and I snatch them out of the air. "Feel free to ask me to babysit it whenever you like. Morning, Jeff."

"Morning, Miss Jones." Jeff's eyes widen with hope at the appearance of a new customer. "Please tell me I can fix you something more interesting than yogurt and berries for breakfast."

Penny—tall, slender, with light brown skin and a halo of dark curls around her beautiful face—fixes her aquamarine eyes on him, and her mouth widens into a bright smile. "Could I have a waffle, with fresh berries as well?"

"Plain, or with chocolate chips?"

"Oh, you devil." Penny drops her messenger bag on the stool next to her with an ominous thud—one that sounds like a fresh load of screenplays for me to pick from. "You know a girl can't resist chocolate chips."

With a devilish grin, Jeff hands me my yogurt and a cup of steaming coffee. Easy service completed, he cracks open an egg and gets to work on the waffle.

"So, what's on the agenda today?" I ask Penny.

"Nah, nah, nah." She shakes her head vigorously. "You can't really expect me not to ask why I needed to buy you a car with half an hour's notice. What was wrong with the Ferrari?"

I shrug noncommittally. "Just trying to evade the paparazzi; you know they have the Ferrari pegged down."

"So why a Tesla? Couldn't you use any of the *twenty* other cars you own?"

"I wanted to try an electric one."

"The I-need-it-in-thirty-minutes-tops text seemed more urgent than that."

I lick yogurt off my spoon. "I can be impatient."

"Oh, come on, boss? I've been racking my brain with all the possibilities since yesterday afternoon. Was it a woman? Did you pick up an ecologist? Someone from the Peace Corps?"

Since I hired her seven years ago, Penny has tried to match me with countless women. Actresses, models, singers, famous, non-famous, she's tried everything. So if I were to tell her I've met someone, she'd bombard me with questions and push the you-need-to-settle-down button nonstop. She means well, of course, but that doesn't stop it from being annoying.

So, no, I'll keep Lana in the closet—so to speak. "Sorry, Penelope, it's strictly confidential."

"Ooooh." My assistant turns toward Jeff. "He called me *Penelope*. It must be serious."

Jeff nods as he places a golden waffle covered in berries and whipped cream in front of her. "He didn't come home for dinner last night."

Penny pops a raspberry into her mouth. "Nothing romantic, Jeff, he was out with Marvin."

"Enough gossip, you two," I interrupt them. "Can I drink my coffee in peace, please? And, yes, *Penelope*, I'd like to know what's on the agenda for today."

Jeff refills my cup and Penny, after hitting me with a we'll-get-back-on-the-topic-later scowl, reads out my schedule for the day. "This morning, you're with me. We have to review potential scripts, then lunch, Liam at four—heads up, he's pissed you stood him up yesterday. But if you told him it was about a woman he might—"

"Enough with this fantasy," I interrupt again. "There is no woman."

She eyes me skeptically. "If you say so."

"Is that all for today?" I ask.

"Only the usual number of dinner invitations to respond to."

"Anything interesting?"

"Indie movie premiere, charity art auction... I have a list if you want to check."

"Sorry, not in the mood to be social."

"Noted. Oh, yes, and Jimmy Kimmel invited you to read a mean tweet."

"Yes to Jimmy, no to the rest." I scoop up the last blueberry and get up. "I'll get dressed and we can start in the office. Jeff, would you mind making another pot of coffee?"

I've got a feeling I'm going to need it; reviewing scripts can be stressful.

"Sure, Mr. Slade."

I nod and turn toward Penny. "I'll be back in five."

"Take your time, boss," she says, forking another generous bite of her waffle. "I'm loving my breakfast."

"Thank you, Miss Jones," Jeff purrs.

I roll my eyes at her; she's always sucking up to the cook, hoping he'll prepare her special treats, which he usually does. For a woman so lean, I've no idea where she puts all the calories. I guess that's twenty-six for you. But pass thirty and, as I painfully discovered a couple of years ago, you pay for every bite.

Aaaand now I'm starting to sound like a desperate real housewife of whatever city.

* * *

When Penny joins me in my home office twenty minutes later, she drops a pile of ten or so scripts—the ones that have already passed her pre-screening—on my desk, sits opposite me, and picks up the top one.

"*Robin Hood* remake," she announces.

I raise an eyebrow. "Another one? Don't screenwriters have any creativity left to develop new characters?"

"The cachet is really interesting."

"Not interested, I want something new," I say.

She drops the script on the desk, laying the foundation of the reject pile. "So I guess it's a no also to a *Pride and Prejudice* remake." She shuffles the scripts and takes out two others. "First installment in the new *Batman* trilogy?"

"I said new."

"But *Batman* is a classic," Penny protests. "And the plot lines are always fresh."

I shake my head.

Penny sighs, puts the two scripts on the no pile, and moves on to the next. "Small town romance."

"Comedy or tearjerker? *Sweet Home Alabama* or *The Notebook*?"

"*Sweet Home Alabama*. It's definitely a happily-ever-after rom-com."

"Title?"

"Love to Hate You."

Ach, so cheesy.

"Plot?"

"In short, a posh city girl gets banished to the country, fights with the local hunk cowboy—*you*—then they fall in love."

I take a deep breath. "Didn't I just tell you I'm tired of doing the same movie over and over again?"

"The story arc might be a trope, but the script is really sassy, and romantic, and will make that tiny part of the female population that's still resisting you capitulate."

"But you know I don't care about that. I want to climb out of the romantic hero box and move on to more serious movies. Matthew McConaughey didn't win the Oscar for *How to Lose a Guy in 10 Days*, he won it for *Dallas Buyers Club*."

"True, but everyone loves him for *How to Lose a Guy in 10 Days*. That's a cult movie, it grossed more than a hundred million in the domestic market, while *Dallas Buyers Club* didn't reach thirty. And *How to Lose a Guy in 10 Days* came out ten years before."

"Exactly. I'm tired of making only commercial movies. I want something more niche."

"And if something interesting and *more niche* comes up, I'll present it to you. That doesn't mean you should give up on the romantic comedy of the year on principle."

I purse my lips.

"Read the script at least," Penny insists. "Then, if you hate it, I won't bring it up again."

"Okay, give it here."

I place the pages in front of me in a new *maybe* pile.

"Next is an epic fantasy. Cool cast, big-bucks budget, and all that jazz."

"Months of shooting?"

"They expect ten."

"Meaning a year or more. Location?"

"A bit in Canada, but it's mostly New Zealand."

I shake my head. "Too much hassle."

The thickest of the manuscripts joins the rejects.

"Dystopian, post-apocalyptic space flick?" Penny asks next.

I repeat the same questions. "How many months of shooting?"

"Seven projected."

"Location?"

"Between here and Vancouver."

"Is the story any good?"

"Wouldn't have suggested it otherwise. And the director is Zander Hughes."

"Oh, I love Zander." I take the bundle from her. "I'll give it a read."

"Great. And last but not least we have three action flicks. You can take your pick of military, spy, and bank robbers."

"Which one's your favorite?"

"Definitely the spy one."

"Okay, leave that script with me and toss the others."

"Perfect." She hands me the last screenplay and stashes the others back in her messenger bag. "You want to move outside?" she asks next. "While you get started on reading those, I can reply to fan mail. It's too much of a beautiful day to stay in."

"And we need our vitamin D," I add jokingly. "Please ask Jeff to bring a jug of OJ to the pool."

In the garden, I settle in the half-shade on a chaise lounge by the infinity pool's edge. Reading assignments in hand, I wait for my freshly squeezed orange juice while musing that there are much harder lines of work.

I love my life.

* * *

"You owe me," Liam says—tall, bald, muscular, of an undecipherable ethnicity that's part African-American, part Asian, with some Caucasian and Latino in the mix—as he marches into the gym, already on the warpath.

"Sorry, mate, I should've warned you I wasn't going to make it yesterday," I say.

"Yeah, you should have. I don't like my time being wasted." My personal trainer steps in front of me. "Let's get to it. Today has to count double. Let's start with dynamic stretching—*arm rotations.*"

I press play on our workout playlist and mirror his movements for the warmup phase.

"So," Liam says. "What was this big emergency you had to stand me up for?"

I didn't want to tell Penny about Lana, but I can be open with Liam. He's been divorced for three years and knows perfectly well what it's like to have everyone he knows try to match him up with that perfect colleague/friend/relative. Plus, he's a bloke; if I tell him there's nothing more to the story, he will listen and forget about the incident tomorrow, not pester me for months with questions.

"I was saving a damsel in distress."

"Oh, yeah?" Liam raises a skeptical eyebrow. "Well, at least you burned some calories—*forward lunges.*"

We stop the arm rotations and lunge forward on alternating legs.

"Sorry, mate, but, no, nothing physical. I was offering only emotional support."

"Oh! Something bad happened to a friend of yours?"

"Nah, I'd just met the lady. Found her crying in a broom closet. A boyfriend-cheating-with-the-best-friend situation."

Liam arches a brow again, questioningly this time. "And what were you doing in a closet? *Lateral squats, to the right, and to the left.*"

"Hiding from the paps. Anyway, I couldn't leave her like that, so I gave her a lift home."

"Nice. You turned her day from 'the day I found out my boyfriend was cheating' to 'the day Christian Slade gave me a ride home'?"

"Nope," I say between squats. "She had no idea who I was."

"Meaning?"

"Apparently she doesn't watch TV."

Liam flashes me a sly smile. "Was she cute?"

"Yeah, she was pretty." More like incredibly beautiful, and with sapphires for eyes. "But it wasn't like that."

"No, no, I get the fascination of meeting someone who doesn't suck up to you from the moment they shake your hand. Must've been refreshing."

"Exactly."

"And I might excuse you on moral grounds, but as your personal trainer, I have to kick your butt instead." He stops the squats. "All right, buddy, let's start with some cardio. One jumping jack, one burpee, push-up at the end, and back up from the top."

As we start jumping, I've no breath left to talk. Also, I take back everything I said before. *I hate my life.*

8

LANA

After Winter leaves, I consider my options. Go to work or call in sick? At well past ten, I'm horrendously late. But turning up late is better than not turning up at all. Plus, the idea of staring at my empty apartment all day is about as appealing as sailing third class to America on the *Titanic*. I'm just going to hit an iceberg of depression and sink. And even if I don't drown right away, I'll freeze to death in the post-break-up waters. Staying at home isn't an option.

I drag my feet to the shower and let the hot water ease my headache. Not bothering with the blow-dryer, I leave my hair wet, pull it into a ponytail secured with a scrunchy Johnathan used to hate and get dressed.

I wear a simple georgette skirt in a floral print and tuck a loose T-shirt into it whose writing summarizes today's mood. The catchphrase is spelled in bold, large characters: I'M A CIVIL ENGI-NEER. Underneath, in smaller font, the punch line: UNLESS YOU MAKE ME ANGRY.

"That's as good as it gets," I tell my mirror image. "Get your ass to work."

I pull on a pair of black flats and am about to reach for the door when I remember the crumpled lab coat I stuffed into my bag yesterday. I usually leave it at work, but now I go to retrieve it and, of course, it's a wrinkled mess. And obviously, the cats slept on it and left it covered in fur.

I'd better fix it. I'm already a woman working in a men-dominated field, the last thing I need is to be tagged as a crazy cat lady as well.

I shove the coat onto a hanger and hook it to my closet door. I retrieve Johnathan's hand steamer from the nook near the bathroom alongside a lint roller and get to work. At least my ex's obsession with pristine clothes is proving useful.

Job done, I drape the lab coat over my shoulder and walk to campus. Since I arrive almost at lunchtime, my fellow researchers regard me with a mix of disdain for showing up late and curiosity.

Ph.D. students aren't exactly known for having a life outside their research. The bunch of detail-oriented, analytical engineers who I share the lab with must be wondering what could've possibly kept me away from the science. Especially considering how early I left yesterday.

"Lana," Trevor, a nice guy focusing his research on reactive flows in combustion systems, whispers.

I walk past him, heading to my station, and pretend I haven't heard. Normally, I'm not this rude. But interacting with another human is more than I can handle right now.

Already, opening up to Winter has left me raw and exposed. I don't want to answer a bunch of personal questions from a colleague I have nothing in common with but a shared interest in high-speed imaging of combustion gases.

I shrug into my lab coat and log in to my computer. I'm about to check my email when someone taps me on the shoulder.

"What?" I turn.

Trevor is staring at me with a taken-aback look at my aggression. I swear I'm usually a nicer person.

"Err, sorry, Voynich, Conway came looking for you an hour ago. He said to send you to his office the moment you turned in."

I close my eyes and take a deep breath. Of course the one day I'm having a personal meltdown, my adviser asks to see me and I'm not at work.

Could he have asked last week when I pulled an all-nighter to finish the paper I had promised him? Nooo. Or two days ago when I came into the lab at 5 a.m. after having a brilliant intuition on why hybrid rocket engines show sub-optimal combustion performance when operating on low-regression-rate fuels. Of course not. It had to be today.

I blink my eyes open and muster my calmest, most-friendly voice. "Thank you, Trevor. Sorry for snapping at you."

He scratches the back of his head. "Nah, no problem. And good luck." He gives me a double thumbs up—totally unironically.

Do I need luck? The well-wishing is more ominous than comforting.

I get up from the stool, grab my notebook from the desk, and stalk off to meet my adviser. His office sits at the end of a long hallway. I amble down it, partly because I'm busy buttoning my lab coat up to my neck, wishing I'd worn a more professional T-shirt to work, and partly because I'm dreading the conversation.

Steven Conway is a good man. He's fair, honest, and incredibly smart. I've spent the last five years working under him, and it's been the best experience of my professional career.

Still, I'm no less worried as I make it to his office and knock on the doorframe since the door is already ajar.

"You wanted to see me, Dr. Conway?"

He looks up from his screen, visibly perturbed. "Ah, Lana. Please, come in. Have a seat."

I take a deep breath, sit down, and set my notebook on my lap.

"Is something wrong?" I'm really hoping the answer is no.

Conway looks up at me, sighs, and puts his hands on his desk. In the two seconds it takes him to complete the action, my brain makes wild guesses as to why he might have asked to see me. Is it the paper I submitted last week? Is something wrong with my research? Or is it yesterday's failed experiment with the high-enthalpy shock tube?

"Yes," he says, confirming my day is about to get worse. "I'm afraid it's bad news."

Don't tell me it's bad news, I want to scream. *Just tell me what it is.*

He must read the anxiousness in my features because he cuts to the chase. "I'm sorry to inform you StaxiaVix filed for bankruptcy last night."

Blood freezes in my veins. StaxiaVix is the aerospace and defense company sponsoring my Ph.D.

"Bankrupt? How? They're a giant, they're..." *too big to fail.*

"Most companies nowadays operate under extenuating circumstances. With a global pandemic, followed by war, inflation, the cost of raw materials going through the roof, and logistic difficulties, many firms weren't able to navigate the storm."

I take his words in, try to accept them.

"What does that mean for me?"

"Your grant has been revoked. You have enough money to cover this year, but need another sponsor for next year."

"Can't the university fund me?"

"The deadline to apply for an internal grant has expired. All fellowships have already been assigned."

"What about NASA? My research is done in collaboration with their Propulsion Jet Lab."

"The perimeter of the financial burden and research scope of the project were detailed with painstaking precision at the beginning of the collaboration." Conway makes an apologetic face. "Trust me, that's not a boat you want to rock."

I grip the plastic chair armrests, trying to ground myself. "What happens if I don't find a sponsor?"

"Your stipend as a teaching assistant would be revoked, you'd have to cover tuition, and you wouldn't have enough funds to conduct more experimental work."

"Tuition? But I signed a contract with the university when I started my doctorate."

"Yes, and like all recipients who are offered other awards from extramural agencies in addition to the fellowship offer from the university, you had to relinquish all Division of Graduate Education-administered awards as students can't hold multiple academic-year stipends exceeding a certain amount."

I wished he'd talk to me more like a human than a bureaucratic cyborg.

"Your grant from StaxiaVix was massive," he continues, and I have to bite my tongue not to reply: *don't I know it?* "It de facto excluded all university funding."

"So if I can't find another sponsor?"

"You'll have to pay for tuition."

"Without a salary."

"Our financial aid department will support you in navigating this new situation. I suggest you make an appointment with an adviser to check what your options are."

Another student loan? I press my fingernails into my palms, trying not to scream. My life is rolling backward. I'll revert to being a penniless student with a ton of debt on her shoulders. Oh gosh. Next, I realize that with Johnathan and his half of the rent gone, I can no longer afford my place, especially if I'm going to be jobless next year. I'll have to go on Craigslist and find new roommates who have no problems living with a couple of hairy cats.

I look back at Conway, who's still politely waiting for me to acknowledge the situation. It's not his fault. I get it. I reached for the sun with the superior grant and now I'm getting burned.

"What am I going to do?" I ask.

"Carry on with your research as planned and make every effort to find a new sponsor. You only have a year left; it shouldn't be too hard. In the meantime, shift your timeline so that you can complete all heavy experimentation work this year. If push comes to shove and we can't come up with alternative funding, you'll already have all the data ready and would only need to analyze it and present it for your final dissertation." He's looking at me with a mixture of pity and positivity. "I'll start hitting all my contacts today. I suggest you do the same."

"Thank you, Dr. Conway."

"Don't thank me yet," he says, then glances at the clock mounted on his wall. "I don't mean to be rude, but I have another student in a different department who was also sponsored by StaxiaVix. She'll be here any minute, and I have to deliver the same piece of bad news to her."

Even if I don't know her, my heart goes out to this fellow researcher whose career aspirations are about to be shattered.

I stand up, pick up my notebook, and try to swallow the lump in my throat. I thank him again and tell him I'll keep him updated. He smiles and shakes my hand. My leave taken, I turn around and head out the door.

As I walk out of his office, my mind is racing, and my heart beating faster. I take a deep breath and try to relax. But I can't. I'm still in shock. What am I going to do? Where will I find the money to pay for school? Even if I get another grant, it most likely won't cover tuition, the stipend, and the research.

I'm not sure if it's the exhaustion, the lack of sleep, or the dizziness spurting from the destruction of everything I cared about in the past twenty-four hours, my relationship first and now my job, but I suddenly feel nauseous. I rush to the bathroom and lock myself in a stall. Crouching down, I place my head between my knees, and try not to throw up.

I stay like that for a few minutes, trying to get my bearings. As the nausea slowly subsides, I lean against the wall and rest my forehead on my tired arms. I stare at the floor, at the shoes of people moving in and out of the restroom, feeling dejected.

And then it hits me: my life is not over. I'm still here and I'm in control. I have the power to make things happen, the ability to make a difference. I'm strong and capable, and I'm not going to give up. I'm going to find a new sponsor and keep my research going.

Resolution made, I sit up straight and take a deep breath. Being a woman in academia is hard; I've been through tough times before and I've come out on top. I'm not going to let this be any different. I won't let adverse circumstances bring me down or define me. I will find a way. I will fight. I'll dig deep and find the resourcefulness I know I have. One way or another, I will make this work.

9

CHRISTIAN

How soon is not too soon to call someone after they've broken up?

Is two weeks enough?

Assuming she dumped the prick.

She must have. Lana didn't strike me as someone who'd stay with a cheater.

Right, but she also didn't look like a woman any man would cheat on.

But most importantly, does she want me to call?

She gave me her business card, true, but I'm not sure it wasn't just a spiteful gesture toward the boyfriend—hopefully ex-boyfriend by now.

Christian, Christian, Christian, why call her? What are you going to do? Invite her to dinner, and then what?

How will you explain the masses of fans, the hordes of paparazzi?

A sure disaster. But it's been two weeks and I haven't been able to push Lana out of my mind...

"Have you finished the screenplays?" Penny's voice brings me back to the here and now of my home office.

I'm tempted to tell her to take the day off and go home. My

fingers are prickling to grab Lana's business card from the desk drawer where I've stashed it and call her, but duty first.

"I have."

"And the verdict?"

"Yes to the rom-com and spy flick, no to the dystopian post-apocalyptic."

"You didn't like the script?"

"No, I did. And Zander is a great director, but I don't want to spend half a year in Vancouver. And since I have the luxury to pick and choose…"

"O-kay." Penny types something on her phone. "Marvin will be disappointed; the post-apocalyptic flick had the highest payoff."

"Marvin lives in Bel Air and drives a Lamborghini, mostly thanks to the commissions he earns on my movies. He'll survive."

"Fair enough."

Her phone pings.

"Yep." Penny turns the screen toward me. "He's sent an unhappy, possibly crying emoji."

FROM MARVIN

I stare at the message and laugh. "Tell him to stop being such a crybaby; he'll still be able to afford his second divorce."

"Is he getting a prenup with wife number three?"

"Should've learned by now."

"I'm not so sure." Penny drums her fingers on my desk. "You know Marvin, he's such a hopeless romantic."

"Yeah, until his assets are cut in half and he has to go on a saving plan to make wife number four happy."

"Why does he keep getting divorced?"

"Falls in love too quickly, gets tired equally fast."

"Isn't wife number two the one leaving him?"

I nod. "Seems the lady was faster than him in realizing the mistake this time around."

"Cheers to happily ever after." Penny laughs sarcastically. "At least Marvin tries to find love..."

And that's my cue to change the subject before the it's-no-longer-cute-to-be-a-bachelor-at-thirty-two speech starts. "Right. Do I have anything scheduled for tonight?"

"Richard and Blair are in town. You're meeting them for dinner."

Richard is one of my oldest friends, from the BH—*Before Hollywood*—era.

"Where to?"

"Verdura. Blair's a vegetarian, remember?"

I didn't.

"Infiltration plan?"

"I've arranged with the manager for you to go in from the kitchen's back door, and you guys will have a private dining room."

"Exfil?"

"Same protocol."

"Perfect."

Penny stares at me in loaded silence.

"What?" I ask.

"Just saying, if Richard found the courage to fall in love again after what happened to him... there's hope for everyone." And before I can even roll my eyes, she adds, "Dying alone is no fun, not even for a Hollywood megastar."

"Are we finished here?"

"Yes, boss."

"Good. I'm going for a swim."

Not sparing another glance at my assistant, I exit the office and abandon Lana's card, along with every intention of calling her. The more I'm pushed toward something, the more I resist.

I'm just wired like that.

* * *

When I arrive at the restaurant that evening, Blair and Richard are already sitting at the table.

"Mate." Richard gets up to greet me, and we hug. "So good to see you."

"You, too." I sit next to Blair—the fiercest, shortest redhead I have ever met—and kiss her on the cheek. "And how's the woman who pulled off the impossible? Never thought I'd see this one settled," I joke, pointing at Richard with my thumb.

"Hasn't been easy," she quips back. "But what can I say? I'm irresistible."

A server arrives with our menus. I notice the surprise in her eyes as she recognizes me, but she recovers quickly enough to announce the day's specials without a hiccup.

As servers' reactions go, the polite overlooking of my persona is my favorite and most rare one. Immediately followed by the moderate fan and, in order of increasing annoyance, the enthusiastic fan, usually put to rest with an autograph or a selfie; the crazy fangirl/boy who either asks too many personal questions, tells me too much about themself or gives me their opinion on every single one of my movies; and, most irritating of all, the aspiring actor who tries to slip me a headshot at the end of the night.

I can never tell when the fan moment will arrive. Sometimes even the most composed servers save a surprise for the check. It can start with a simple "Call me" followed by their phone number written on the bill and escalate from there to the most indecent of proposals. But at least at that point, I'm already leaving. Anyway, that's why I prefer house parties: more privacy.

And also better food.

I stare at the menu, disheartened.

"Mmm, Blair?" I ask. "Do you have any suggestions? I'm not much of a veggie person."

"You like strong cheeses?"

"Yeah?"

"Then try the gorgonzola and walnut pasta, it's delicious."

I eye the menu, still unconvinced. Nuts and pasta don't seem like a good pairing. "What are you getting, mate?" I ask Richard.

"Yeah, the pasta is delicious," Richard answers distractedly.

"I need the restroom," Blair says, standing. Even if she's wearing five-inch killer heels, she's still super short, and adorably so, but never tell her that or she might bite your head off. "If the server comes back to take our orders, I'll have the eggplant parmigiana."

As she walks away, I turn to Richard. "What's up with you? Are you okay?"

"Sorry, Chris, I'm distracted."

"I gathered that. By...?"

"I'm not really in LA to meet investors for the magazine," Richards explains. He's the founder and editor-in-chief of an online-only news outlet.

"Oh, and the plot thickens. So, what's the covert mission?"

Richard takes his time unfolding his napkin over his legs. "I haven't told anyone, so you can't let it show on your face."

"Not to worry, I'm a pretty good *actor*," I tease as our server comes back with our drinks.

Despite my doubts, I order the pasta. Richard as well. He adds Blair's parmigiana, and once the server's gone, I wait for him to tell me what the big secret is.

My friend takes a generous sip of red wine and then says, "I'm proposing to Blair tomorrow."

POW!

Richard drops the bomb without preamble.

"Really?"

"Yeah, I have the grand gesture all planned at Griffith Observatory."

"I... I'm... Wow!" I stutter. "I thought you were done with weddings."

"Me too, but Blair, she's... she's..."

"She's made you lose your mind," I offer.

"Pretty much." Richard's face brightens with a goofy smile. "But in a good way."

"I'm so happy for you, mate." I slap him on the shoulder. "And this time I'll be there no matter if I'm in the middle of shooting a movie in Australia."

"You'd better be because I've got a feeling this time I'll actually end up married by the end of the ceremony."

"Look at you, so sure she'll say yes, you arrogant bastard!"

"I hope so."

Here comes the goofy smile again.

"Why propose in LA?" I ask. "New York wasn't romantic enough for you?"

"LA was our first trip together when I realized she wasn't just an employee, so to speak."

"Yeah, but you didn't tell her then, right?"

"No, but just because I was still being a tosser," Richard says gravely. "LA is where everything started, at least for me, and I hope Blair will focus on that."

I raise my glass. "To you, mate."

Richard clinks his glass against mine just as Blair comes back from the restroom.

"What are you guys toasting?"

I see the panic on Richard's face and promptly come to the rescue. "My next blockbuster. Signed the contract today." Which is not even a lie.

"Oh, what's the movie about?" Blair asks, then quickly adds, "If you're at liberty to say..."

"Am I off the record?"

She smiles. "With us? Always!"

"It's a small-town romance, with an infuriatingly charming leading man who falls for the out-of-her-element city girl."

"Sounds..."

"Like it's been done a million times before?"

"Not what I was going to say, but, yeah, it has been done a million times before."

"True, but the script was too clever to pass on. Trust me, it'll be a huge success."

"Oh, I'm not complaining. I'd eat romcoms for dinner every night if I could." She smiles and takes a sip of wine. "How about real-life romances? Where's the woman who never watches TV?"

I almost choke on my wine. How can she know about Lana? I haven't told anyone about her. Okay, yes, I did tell Liam... but I seriously doubt he and Blair know each other.

"How do you know?" I ask.

Blair frowns. "Know what?"

"About Lana."

"Lana? Who's Lana?"

"You asked me where she was?"

Her confusion deepens. "No, I asked how it was going with your search for... *oh!*"

Comprehension dawns on her as the shoe drops for me, too: she's referring to our conversation about dating from the Teachers Without Postcodes charity gala last year.

Now Blair smiles shrewdly. "You mean you've actually found a woman who has no clue who you are?"

I lean back in my chair. I'm so busted.

"I'm not following," Richard says. "What are you guys talking about?"

Blair turns toward him to explain. "Last year at the charity gala, Christian spent the whole night telling me all about the hardships of dating as Hollywood's most wanted bachelor and told me the only way for him to find his one true love would be to meet a woman who had no idea who he was whatsoever." She pauses for effect. "And it seems now he's finally found her, and she has a name: Lana."

They both stare at me expectantly, but I'm saved from replying by the server arriving with our dishes. The conversation dies down as we all take our first bites.

"How's your pasta?" Blair asks after a while.

And despite my initial prejudice, I have to say, "Pretty amazing."

"So." A little, evil smile dances on her lips. "This mystery woman... You really didn't think we forgot about her, right? And before you ask, yeah, you're off the record."

I sigh and tell them how Lana and I met. When I finish the story, Richard still seems too nervous or too absorbed in his own love troubles to comment, but Blair is enthusiastic.

"Wow, if that's not a meet-cute worthy of a movie! Have you called her yet?"

"Nah."

"But why?"

"It happened only two weeks ago. Isn't it too short a time to get over a ten-year relationship?"

Blair takes a sip of wine. "Depends on if she was still in love with the dude or not."

"She was pretty upset."

"Of course she was upset. Being cheated on is no fun, whether you're still in love or not," Blair says passionately. Is she talking from personal experience? I seem to remember there was a story there involving spaghetti marinara, but before I can pin down the memory, she continues with her speech. "And you also have to factor in the best friend aspect. That alone would be enough to upset anyone."

"How long after your last breakup did you meet Richard?" I ask.

Blair beams and turns to Richard. "Twenty minutes? Half an hour, tops?"

They lock eyes and share a complicit smile. Such a simple gesture, and yet so full of hidden meaning. The mirror of a deeper connection, of a partnership, of shared inside jokes, of intimacy... They're so clearly and completely in love with each other that it makes my stomach ache with longing. I've never had a bond that real, and until just now, I also hadn't realized how much I yearned for it. Penny might be onto something. Not that I'll ever tell her that.

"But to be fair." Blair breaks eye contact with Richard and returns her attention to me. "I don't remember much of the night in question. Anyway, breakup time is meaningless; it's depth of feelings you want to look out for."

"Of that, I've no idea."

"Only one way to find out. You should call her."

"Mmm..."

"Richard, tell Christian he should call the mystery woman."

My friend gives me a blank stare and says, "Definitely."

He's so spaced out that Blair could've asked him if he wanted triplets and he would've given the same answer.

Still, the night leaves me with a sense of deep unease.

At home, before I go to bed, I step into the office and take Lana's card out of the desk drawer.

To call or not to call?

10

LANA

"Excuse me, Professor?" a male student calls.

"Yeah," I say, turning toward the classroom.

"Aren't Navier-Stokes equations supposed to be partial derivatives?" the nerdy-looking boy with thick glasses and a mop of curly carrot-orange hair asks from the second row.

I blink back at the board and notice I've used the wrong differential symbol in all the equations.

"Good catch, Montgomery."

Mortified, I start to erase all the dx symbols and substitute them with δ. Gosh, there's, like, a million of the little buggers.

"Sorry, guys, I'm having a rough couple of weeks."

I turn to the class to find my intermediate fluid dynamics undergrads staring back at me with blank expressions as if I've said something incomprehensible. As if TAs weren't supposed to have lives outside the classroom.

"Anyway..." I smile awkwardly, and, oh boy, I'm blushing. I hope the students will interpret it as a simple I've-messed-up-my-differential-equations embarrassment and not a my-personal-and-professional-lives-are-in-ruins shame. "As I was saying, Navier-

Stokes equations describe how the velocity, pressure, temperature, and density of a moving fluid are related..."

When the class ends, I'm relieved. At least until I remember that going home after work now only means packing what remains of my life in loser-who-has-to-move-in-with-a-friend boxes.

When I told Winter about my new precarious financial situation, she immediately offered to room with me. Her apartment has a spare bedroom, and she reassured me she'd be happy for me and the cats to move in. Initially, she tried to have me stay with her rent-free, but I refused. Accepting charity from friends and family is where I draw the line. And anyway, half the rent at her apartment is cheaper than what I was paying with Johnathan for our house. And even if it weren't, the idea of moving in with strangers was so unappealing that I would've said yes anyway.

My landlord has been incredibly understanding in dissolving the lease early. Especially since I found him replacement tenants, so that he won't lose a single month of income. My house is going to a colleague who wanted to move closer to campus. He still has his grant and has no money issues. Winter's place is not as close. I won't be able to walk to work anymore and will have to use public transportation. But I'm not about to look a gift horse in the mouth. I'll get to live in a clean, beautiful apartment with the perfect roommate. Given the cringe ads I'd found on Craigslist before Winter offered up her place, I count myself lucky. Not just for having found a place to live, but mostly for sharing it with my remaining best friend.

It's been two weeks since I kicked Johnathan out of the house and I'm still not used to the silence. Even if I wasn't madly in love with my boyfriend anymore, I still can't erase the empty crater he's left in my life as easily as swiping an eraser across a chalkboard.

Weekends are no better. So far I've gone out only once, socially, and it was as awkward as I'd expected. Everyone in our group was tiptoeing around me, and the absence of Summer and Johnathan was as conspicuous as the side glances and pitiful stares my friends kept throwing at me. Everyone did their best to be cheerful and upbeat and easygoing, but they were trying so hard they ended up being exactly the opposite. The only enjoyable parts of my weekends so far have been my tutoring sessions at the charter school where I volunteer.

Once the last of my students have left the classroom, I shoulder my messenger bag and head out myself. I should stop by the lab and check my emails, but the idea of opening another grant rejection letter is too disheartening. Equally depressing is the idea of going back to my empty house stashed with half-packed boxes. So instead, I stop at my neighborhood's public library.

Books have always been my greatest comfort and escape from reality. The feeling of sinking into a novel, of being wholly immersed in a different world, is a lifeline for me. In fiction, my troubles become irrelevant. Stories are where I can escape the pain and emptiness of my life, even if it's only for a few hours.

"Hello, Marjory," I greet my favorite librarian as soon as I push past the glass revolving doors.

She's wearing a plain T-shirt with the words 'Dinosaurs didn't read, they're now extinct' splashed across the middle that immediately cheers me up.

"Hi, Lana," she says back. About my age, with wavy light-brown hair and hazel eyes, Marjory is my go-to gal for book recommendations. "Already finished with the pirate story?"

"Yeah," I confirm.

"And what are you in the mood for today?"

"I want something epic—literally." I smile. "With castles, and princesses, and knights in shining armor."

"Oooh, how exciting. Are we talking historical fiction or epic fantasy?"

"Either," I say. "Whichever has the better story."

"Let me check our online catalog." Marjory picks up a tablet from her desk and taps the screen a few times. "If you'd like to browse in the meantime, fantasy is in aisle eight and historical fiction at four."

I thank her and begin to stroll around the library, fascinated by the endless orderly rows of titles. I never borrow physical copies of books; I come here only to get recommendations, and then I check out the eBook on the library website and download the file on my eReader. Mostly because I think we humans should stop chopping down forests to print books. If bookworms all over the world switched to digital reading, it'd save so many trees.

Still, being a book lover, I'm not immune to the allure of holding a real book in my hands and, yes, occasionally smelling the pages.

While I give Marjory time to come up with a few suggestions, I get my fix of smelling newer-looking paperbacks, read the first few pages, snap pictures of the covers of books I might like, and finally go back to Marjory to hear her opinion.

"Did you find anything?" she asks.

I show her the pics. "What do you think of these two?"

She stares at the first cover. "This one was a *meh* for me, but you can always check it out and return it if you don't like it." Marjory swipes left to the next picture. "Oh, and this one is amazing, but it's a five-book series of pretty hefty tomes, so unless you're in the mood to spend a few months in the fantasy middle ages... Actually, you're a quick reader so one month might be enough for you. Anyway, once you start with this"—she now makes a funny, deeper monster voice—"you really have to commit."

"It's a no, then," I say. Lately, I like to change genre with every book I read. I've been stuck doing too much of the same for the past ten years and now I want to keep things fresh—literarily, at least. "What do you have for me?"

"Two nice standalones." She pulls up the covers on her tablet. "This one's set in Middle Ages England and features star-crossed lovers, battles, intrigue, politics... And this one is basically the same, but with magic and a few fantastic creatures added into the mix."

"They both sound wonderful." I add the two titles to my wish list. "I'll decide at home, depending on how magically inclined I feel."

"Glad I could help. It's always a pleasure seeing you, Lana."

"You, too, Marjory. Bye."

I'm exiting the library when Marjory calls, "Hey, Lana, wait up!"

I turn to see her walking toward me.

"Here's my phone number." She hands me a pink Post-it note. "Give me a call when you have the chance; we could grab a coffee and talk more about books."

Her eyes are all shiny, her smile bright and warm.

"Wow, thanks," I say, grabbing the card.

"I'm sorry." Marjory's smile falters a little. "Am I being too forward? It's just that it's so rare to meet someone who loves books as much as I do. I thought we could be friends, but if you don't want to—"

"No," I interrupt her, smiling. "You're right. I wonder why I never thought of asking you. Coffee sounds great. I'll text you my number so we can pick a date."

"Perfect." She pulls me into a quick hug. "I can't wait."

This is what I need, I think on the way home. To meet new people, have new friends. Kudos to Marjory for taking the initiative; I would've never asked her to grab a coffee with me. Which makes no sense, as it's a great idea. I need to borrow a page out of her book—*pun intended*—and be more proactive. New friends won't drop into my lap from the sky, not if I don't get out there and seek them. Maybe I should join a book club.

I'm in the process of googling "how to find the right book club for you" as I walk into my house. It keeps me distracted for a while until my stomach growls and I realize I'm starving. Grabbing the takeout menu off the fridge, I tap in the number for the pizza place and order a medium all-dressed.

Excluding high school puppy love, I've only ever been in a serious relationship with Johnathan. And he was the cook of the house. Since he's been gone, I've been ordering takeout almost every night—which is super bad for my health and anti-economic. But like books, I need a bit of comfort food right now and I hope all the walking I do will burn off the extra calories. So far I haven't gained weight, but I should add *learn how to cook on YouTube* to the *my new life as a single, destitute woman* list of things to do.

"*Meow.*"

"*Meeoow.*"

The cats remind me it's dinnertime for them as well.

"Hello, kitties." I grab a can of cat food from the cabinet. "How was your day?"

The loud purring I receive in response has nothing to do with me and everything to do with the food they're about to get. But thank goodness for Cengel and Boles; without them, the total emptiness of the house would've been too depressing.

I feed the cats and then sit back at the bar, reading the blurbs of the two books Marjory suggested. I'm halfway into the first one when my phone beeps and a message from Winter appears on the top half of the screen.

FROM WINTER

How's it going?

I'm teaching a beginner photography class next month

You should totally join

My first instinct is to reply, yeah, count me in. But then I remember I probably can't afford any extras at the moment.

TO WINTER

I'd love to, but at the moment I have to save every penny I can

FROM WINTER

Don't be silly, I'm not making you pay the enrolment fee

TO WINTER

I already told you accepting handouts makes me feel horrible

FROM WINTER

This wouldn't be a handout, it'd be me sharing what I love the most with my best friend while a bunch of strangers pays me for it

Say yes, please

TO WINTER

I don't even own a camera

FROM WINTER

I'll lend you one of my old ones

Please say yes

I love how Winter never gives up.

TO WINTER

Okay, I'm in

FROM WINTER

Really? I'm so happy

You're gonna love it

I'll text you the info once the final dates are fixed

TO WINTER

Thank you, I need to try new things

FROM WINTER

You're going to love photography, I promise

TO WINTER

Love you

FROM WINTER

💜 u too

A book club, virtual cooking classes, a beginner photography course, and with my new friend Marjory on the horizon, I should have enough distractions not to get too depressed about my cheating ex-boyfriend and derailing career. Sometimes bad situations resolve themselves. Something will come up. I've inquired with so many institutions for sponsorship, one of them will come through.

Mid-let's-be-positive-about-the-future pep talk, Boles jumps onto the stool next to mine. I scratch him under the chin and smile to myself for the first time in what feels like forever.

Old, mopey Lana, bye-bye. New, positive Lana, ready to conquer the world.

* * *

I've just paid the delivery boy and settled down with my pizza when my phone rings again. A call from an unknown number.

With a thrill of curiosity, I say, "Hello?"

"Lana?" a male voice asks.

My heart sinks a little. If it were someone responding to a grant application they would've addressed me by my surname.

"Yes. Who's speaking?"

"Christian, from the Peninsula's closet."

At once my pulse picks up—if not a grant offer, a handsome stranger calling is the next best thing. "Oh. Hi?"

"Just checking on you, in case you were hiding again in a store-room somewhere and needed rescuing."

I chuckle. "No, not hiding anywhere, but thank you for checking."

"Am I interrupting something?"

"Only my solo dinner," I say, adding a flirty note to my voice.

If old Lana thought Christian was trouble, new Lana is open to... experiment...

"Any interest in a non-solo dinner?" he asks. "I mean, you want to grab a bite together? If... if it's not too soon."

"No."

"Oh, okay."

He sounds downcast.

"I meant, yes to dinner, no, it's not too soon."

Dating someone new might not be the best choice for me right now, not with all the effort I'll need to pour into work if I want to keep my sinking-career boat afloat. But I also have to consider my mental health. Locking myself in a shell, thinking about work and the upcoming doom twenty-four-seven is no good. I need to get out more. See new people. Smile more. And Christian sounds like a good time.

"Great." I can practically hear the smile in his voice. "Would Thursday night work for you?"

"Yes, I'd love to."

"Pick you up at seven-ish?"

"You remember where I live?"

"Yeah."

"Perfect. See you Thursday, then."

I hang up with a silly smile stamped on my face, and I don't even care that my pizza has gone cold in the meantime.

11

CHRISTIAN

Christian, you moron.

What have I done? Inviting Lana to dinner was a stupid idea. What am I going to do when we show up at a restaurant and a mob assaults us demanding selfies and autographs? I'm an idiot. I should call her back and cancel.

No, I want to go on a date with Lana!

So what now?

I could invite her here and have Jeff make dinner.

Yeah, 'cause the mansion would be so much less of a giveaway than a crowd of fans.

What if I rented a more understated Airbnb and still have Jeff prepare our meal?

Nah, too much of a lie.

Or I could buy a smaller house and invite her there.

Still too dishonest.

What else? What else?

Then the perfect idea hits me.

It's romantic, private, and I'm a genius.

* * *

"Bill," I say into the intercom on Thursday, calling my driver and garage manager—and, yeah, owning over twenty cars I need a garage manager. I wouldn't be able to keep up with insurance payments, maintenance, and so on otherwise. "Can you please bring up the Tesla?"

"Right away, sir." Bill's voice comes back distorted over the speaker.

"The Tesla, huh?" Penny echoes.

She's still here in my office collecting her stuff before she goes home for the day.

"You have something against that car?"

"No, boss." She puts her laptop away and loops her messenger bag over her shoulder. "It's just that since you had me buy the Tesla, you haven't driven it once... until now."

"So?"

"I manage your schedule, and there's nothing on the agenda for tonight."

Ah. Busted. Sort of.

"Can't a guy go for a drive in his car?"

"A guy can, but a certain Sexiest Man Alive who hates driving around LA for fear of the paparazzi..."

Ha-ha, she's given me the perfect excuse. "That's why I'm taking the Tesla. To stay incognito." Penny rolls her eyes and refuses to engage further, so, of course, I prompt her. "What?"

"Boss, you pick your cars based on how much noise they make... and you can keep denying it as long as you want, but I know something is up with that car." She pauses and smirks. "I can only hope it's about a woman. I like her already."

I give her my no-comment face and, as soon as she leaves—still sporting that annoying, know-it-all grin—I go upstairs to shower.

An hour later—thirty minutes to get ready plus thirty minutes of LA traffic—I'm pulling up in front of Lana's house.

To be polite, I should walk to her door, ring the bell, and wait for her on the doorstep. But too many people are still walking around and the sun hasn't set yet—I should hope since I've planned a sunset date—so getting out of the car is too big of a risk. What if someone recognizes me?

Instead, I text Lana to let her know that I'm here.

She comes out of the house five minutes later wearing a bright, flowy dress in a colored flower print. Her hair is loose and, as it catches the late-afternoon light, the dark brown shines with a hint of chocolate undertones.

Risky or not, I'm not completely ungracious; I at least get out of the Tesla to open the car door for her. The gesture earns me a big smile and a quick, hello-you hug.

As Lana wraps her arms around my chest, I inhale a fresh, floral, fruity fragrance that goes perfectly with her dress. She smells like a blooming flower garden.

Lana lets go of me and smiles again. "Thank you for picking me up."

"Are you kidding? No problem at all."

I close the car door for her and quickly regain the driver's seat, keeping my head low the entire time lest someone spots me.

As I pull away from the curb, there's a moment of awkward silence until we both speak at once.

"So how have you been?" I ask, just as Lana says, "I'm glad you called the other night."

And we also reply at the same time.

"I'm glad I called, too," I say, as Lana blushes and counters, "I'm hanging in there, but it's not all been negative."

"You've moved on from the breakup already?" I talk alone this time.

"Wow." Lana turns to me, but I keep staring at the road. "Straight to the punch."

"Too direct?" I dare a peek at her; Lana's expression is still open and warm. "I thought it'd be best if we got rid of the pink elephant right away."

"I, too, would like for things to be straightforward between us, but can I ask for a glass of wine before we talk exes?" She gives me a small smile that I still find brighter than the California sun. "I assume they have wine where we're going?"

I grin. "They don't, actually, but I hope the scenery will compensate for the lack of alcohol."

Lana frowns at first, then shrugs. "Probably better, on second thought. I'm too much of a lightweight, anyway."

I chuckle.

Lana is special. Not only is she breathtakingly beautiful in the simplest way, but she has wit, and a down-to-earth, no-BS pragmatism so different from what I'm used to in the smoke and mirrors games of Hollywood. All qualities I find hard to resist. Not that I have to.

Thirty minutes later, as per usual LA dreadful mobility, I'm helping Lana out of the car near a friend's house in Malibu.

She looks around the row of beachfront mansions, perplexed. "Is there a restaurant here?" she asks.

"Not exactly." I smile.

From the trunk of the Tesla, I grab two blankets and the picnic basket Jeff prepared.

"Wow." Lana claps her hands. "We're going on a picnic?"

"I hope you don't mind it's not a traditional dinner?"

"Oh, no. I love it."

Relieved by her enthusiasm and with my hands full, I beckon Lana to follow me with a lift of my chin and guide her past my friend's driveway to the beach's access point.

"Are you sure we're allowed here?" Lana asks, pointing at the big sign marking the entryway.

RIGHT TO PASS
BY PERMISSION
AND SUBJECT
TO CONTROL
OF OWNER
SECTION 1008, CIVIL CODE

"Those signs are bogus," I reply cheerfully. "The beach is public everywhere."

I also have secured permission from said owner just in case.

We walk past the house, and our feet touch the sand just as the sun begins to lower over the horizon. Lana helps me spread the blanket evenly on the ground, and we sit on the soft fabric facing the ocean.

I unpack everything Jeff arranged—a selection of cheeses, cold cuts, fruit, and sandwiches cut into small triangles—lay the food on the blanket and grab two glasses.

"As per California drinking rules," I announce, "our beverage choices include apple cider, water, or iced peach tea."

"Iced tea would be great, thanks."

I hand Lana a glass and fill mine with tea as well, saying, "We should toast."

"To?"

"Hotel supply rooms?"

Lana chuckles, clinks her glass against mine, and takes a small sip. Then she glues those impossibly blue eyes of hers on me. "So, my ex. What did you want to know?"

"How you're coping, I guess, and..." My palms go sweaty. *Wow,*

takes more guts to say this than I expected. "If you're open to something new?"

Lana lowers her gaze and blushes.

"I'm okay, all things considered," she finally says.

I wait for her to tell me more.

"My other best friend..." she continues. "My two best friends
are twins; did I mention it?"

"Nope."

"Well, they are." Lana winces, adding, "Anyway, the non-evil
twin made me take an honest look at my relationship with
Johnathan."

"And?"

"I realized I wasn't in love with him anymore. Hadn't been for a
long time. An obvious fact to everyone but me, apparently." Lana
pushes a lock of hair behind her ear and takes another sip of tea.
"Deep down, I knew my feelings weren't as intense as in the beginning, but Johnathan had been such a given in my life, I never
stopped for one second to question our status. I really don't blame
him for ending our relationship, only for the way he did it. We
could've handled the situation like two reasonable adults, but
finding out he was sleeping with my best friend behind my back
sort of nixed that."

So far I couldn't hope for a better answer. "How did that night
go, after I left your home?"

"It was all very civilized." Her secret smile makes an appearance. "Sort of."

"Meaning?"

"I may or may not have packed all his clothes in a crumpled
mess and let the cats take a nap in the suitcases before closing
them." The smile widens. "Because who doesn't like a side of cat
hair with their wrinkled shirts?"

I can't help but laugh my head off. "Not so bad as revenge goes."

"No, I agree. Anyway, when Johnathan got home, I told him I wanted him gone. He was upset—that I'd caught him, not for what he did—and that was it. He loaded his stuff into the car and left. Haven't heard from him since."

"And your friend?"

Lana's mouth presses in a tough line before she replies, making it apparent the betrayal from her friend stung more than that of her ex. "Her twin sister gave me the list of run-of-the-mill excuses Summer used to defend herself, but she hasn't reached out. Must be too ashamed or too much of a coward to face me."

"Would you want her to?"

"An apology would be nice." Lana collects a little mound of sand and lets the grains slip through her fingers. "But I don't know if I'll ever be able to forgive her. They scrambled my entire social life. Johnathan, Summer, and I were part of such a close group of friends. We'd been a tight band since college, but now it's ruined. Everyone's awkward, they're all picking sides. No one condones their actions, but it's not like Johnathan's best friend will choose me over him because of that, and the best friend's wife goes with him... You get the picture."

"I do."

Lana gives me an intense stare. "Have you ever... been cheated on?"

"Oh, yeah."

"How did you find out?"

Read it on a tabloid cover.

"Someone saw them together," I say instead. "Not my highest moment."

"Were you in love with her?"

"I'm not even sure anymore. It was years ago." After so long, I only remember the anger at my private life being the center of a nationwide scandal. Having my face, her face, and the other bloke's face plastered on magazine covers for over a year. But I don't tell Lana any of this; I can't. If she finds out who I am, the magic will be gone. And I don't want this thing between us—whatever it is—to end.

"Anyway," I continue, "she wasn't right for me. In hindsight, it's easy to tell. But, like you, I would've preferred for things to end differently. To avoid everything that came as a package deal with the breakup, everybody knowing I had been cheated on, and the sympathy..."

"Oh, the sympathy is the worst," Lana agrees. "But at least he wasn't your best friend, I hope?"

"No, never met the guy."

Only saw him on TV. Years later, we're still on each other's blacklists; can't be invited to the same events. And thankfully, his name gets crossed off the list more often than mine. It's all about the small victories.

"But to end the past relationships talk," Lana says, "my point is that even if I'm over my ex emotionally, I'm not adjusted to the breakup yet. Still a bit socially awkward."

"A toast." I raise my glass. "To cheating exes who can no longer hurt us, and to new beginnings."

12

LANA

Gosh, his eyes are the color of the ocean. At first, I thought they were more green, but staring at them now in the dying sunlight they have intense blue in them, too, deep and electric colors all mixed into one. The more Christian stares at me, the more my cheeks heat up. Shoot, I'm blushing, and for no reason at all.

As a diversion, I clink my glass against his. "To new beginnings," I repeat, and to distract myself, I grab one of the mini sandwiches and stuff it in my mouth. "Wow, these are delicious." The taste of smoked salmon mixes with rocket leaves and a spice I don't recognize. "What did you put in them?"

"I have a confession to make."

Oh, no. He's making that cute face again, with the small frown and a hint of a crooked smile, and my cheeks are hotter than ever.

"What?" I ask.

"I didn't really make the sandwiches; I ordered them. I'm not the best around the kitchen."

"Oh, no," I say. "Then we're doomed."

The cute frown deepens. "Why?"

"I can't cook," I explain. "If you can't cook, either, how are we ever going to eat?"

Christian makes a weird face as if he's choking back the first answer that popped into his head.

"We could always learn," he says eventually.

"Oh, I plan to." I pause to swallow the last bit of the mini sandwich. "I've looked at cooking classes online but haven't decided on one yet. You ever thought about taking a cooking class?"

"Yeah, sure."

He doesn't seem enthusiastic.

"Not a fan of cooking?" I ask.

"No, I'd love to learn," Christian says. But something still seems off, and he changes the subject quickly. "What else has been going on with you?"

A reminder of the grant apocalypse slams into my chest like a heavy stone. I try to hide the worry from my face and grab a slice of cheese before I answer him, choosing to concentrate on the positive. "I'm moving in with my best friend. Now that Johnathan's gone, I can no longer afford the rent on my own." No need to add that I might be out of a job next semester and could end up having wasted the last five years of my life on a doctorate I won't be able to complete if I don't get approved for a student loan.

"The non-evil twin, right?" Christian asks.

"Yeah, Winter."

"What else?"

"I plan to learn new things, try different experiences, meet new people..."

"New people, plural?"

"Yeah, why?"

His face falls. "So you're dating someone else, too?"

"No, no." I blush ten times harder than before. "I'm seeing only you that way. But I have a new friend. Her name is Marjory; she's my favorite librarian. I've known her forever but never hung out with her outside the library." I'm aware I'm over-explaining, but when I'm nervous, I talk. "The other day she invited me for coffee and I said, wow, yeah, why have I never thought of that? So we're meeting tomorrow afternoon for the first time. And that's me, learning to cook, taking a photography class, making new friends..."

"Dating me," Christian says with a cheeky smile.

And I don't think my face can become any redder.

"What about you?" I ask. "Have you been single long?"

"Yes, it's been a while."

"How come?"

"It's hard to find the right person. And I suppose I have trust issues."

"Why? Because of what happened with your ex?"

Christian frowns like he knows what he wants to say but is having trouble expressing the concept in so many words.

"In part. But in all my past relationships I've always felt like the other person had more at stake than just being with me..."

I'm not sure how to read this answer. "Really? Like what?"

A shadow passes over his face. "Oh, this and that..."

Clearly, Christian is not comfortable discussing this particular topic. I'm curious, but I let the subject drop. I want tonight to stay light, and we've already discussed our exes enough.

So my next question is about something else entirely. "How about your secret movie project? You sorted it out with your partners?"

"Oh, that. I'm still working on it."

That shadow again. As soon as I ask something personal or try to dig a little deeper into his life, the shadow arrives. I'm all for the brooding, mysterious hero, but at this pace, Christian is going to stay a blank page for me. A very attractive blank page, though.

Okay, buddy, last chance.

"How come you have a British accent? Did you grow up in England?"

Ding-ding-ding.

Jackpot!

I finally get a smile out of him.

And from that moment on, the conversation flows between us. Christian tells me everything about growing up in London while traveling often to the States to see his mother's family. He talks about the British stuff he misses here in LA—not the weather, and not the British humor.

Time flies as we eat the sandwiches and drink the tea. I could listen to his deep, sexy voice for hours. And the ocean setting is so romantic... Even with the sky darkening fast now, the mansions behind us glitter like fairy lights.

And Christian, he's... he must come from another planet. Really, they don't make men this handsome on Earth. And he's also fun. He tells me a couple of terrible British jokes so horrendous they become funny.

"So that was me before moving to LA," he concludes. "What about you? Are you from around here?"

"Yeah, although my life hasn't been half as glamorous as yours. I grew up in Pasadena and moved here for college when I was eighteen."

"To study aerospace engineering."

"Correct."

"Why? You wanted to be an astronaut?"

"True, you need a STEM degree to become an astronaut. But that's not why I chose engineering. I mean, astronauts drink recycled pee." I make a disgusted face. "That alone would be enough never to make a go at outer space."

"Second that."

"I picked engineering for a much simpler reason. In high school, I excelled at math, but I don't like theoretical studies, so engineering seemed like the best practical application."

"So you like to build things?"

"And make scientific discoveries, prove new theories, break the boundaries of what's possible." As I remember once again that that might not be in the cards for me anymore, that all my hard work could amount to nothing, the smile drops from my face and I'm not quick enough to hide the worry.

"Hey," Christian says in the softest voice. "What's the matter?"

"Oh, nothing."

But he's no fool. "Looks like something."

I don't see the point of keeping it secret from him, he's already seen me at my lowest and hasn't judged or pitied me for a second. No matter that I don't know him that well, he's one of the few people I feel comfortable talking about my job with, or potential lack thereof.

"I ran into a hiccup at work. The company sponsoring my Ph.D. went belly up, so my funding for next academic year isn't secure unless I can find a new donor."

"Doesn't the university support its researchers?"

"They would have if I hadn't accepted a larger grant from an external agency. And now it's too late to apply for a university-sponsored fellowship."

"I'm sorry."

"Don't be. It's only March." I downplay the gravity of the situation and try to put it out of my head. I don't want real life to intrude tonight. "I still have time until the fall quarter begins."

"I'm sure you'll find someone."

"Yeah," I say, wrapping my arms around my chest and shivering a little in the night breeze. Since the sun went down, it started getting chilly.

"Come here," Christian says, noticing I'm getting cold. "I have an extra blanket."

I snuggle close to him, and he wraps the blanket around both our shoulders. And suddenly, the fact that I'm on a date for the first time in ten years hits me. I blush and can't bear to keep eye contact with Christian, so I look up at the stars.

"They're beautiful," Christian whispers. "Aren't they?"

"Mm-hm."

"Makes you wonder how far away they are."

"Well, the sun is the closest star to Earth at about 150 million kilometers. While the farthest star known to humankind is Icarus, a whopping 9 billion light years away."

"Wow." Christian low whistles. "Telescopes can see that far? I had no idea."

"Not really. Astronomers could only spot Icarus because of the gravitational lensing given by a far-off supernova."

"The gravi-what?"

"Sorry for getting so technical." I turn to him. Gosh, our faces are so close, I would only have to lean in an inch for our lips to touch. "Am I boring you?"

"No, I'm fascinated."

I'm not sure if he's playing nice or if he's really interested, but I explain the phenomenon to him anyway. "*Gravitational lensing*: it happens when gravity from a massive celestial object, like the explosive death of a giant star, acts as a magnifying glass..."

Christian looks weirded out.

"Sorry." I lower my gaze self-consciously. "Definitely too technical?"

"No." Christian gently lifts my chin with one hand. "I'm awed by how smart and knowledgeable you are."

Eyes burning into mine, he pulls me closer, cups my cheek in a delicate caress, and bends down to kiss me.

His lips are soft but demanding. There's the light scratch of his stubble against my skin, and, help me, because it feels like a giant star is having its explosive death inside my belly. Leave it to me to grow a supernova instead of the customary butterflies.

Christian lays me down, the sand underneath acting as soft bedding. "You're so beautiful," he whispers. "I feel like the luckiest man in the world."

In response, I lift up to kiss him again but he pulls away. "Stop me if I'm going too fast. It's only been two weeks; we don't have to do anything you're uncomfortable with."

I can hear the tension underlying his words, the hope and fear they convey. I'm not sure I'm ready to go all the way, not after ten years of only being with one person. But I know I want to kiss Christian.

"I'm fine with kissing," I say.

His mouth finds mine again, and this time, it's more passionate. His hands move to my waist and I can feel the heat radiating between us. I tilt my head, and Christian deepens the kiss. His hands move up my sides and his fingers entwine in my hair. The entire universe compressed into this moment.

"You still okay?" Christian rasps.

I nod and pull him toward me another time. We kiss for a long time, letting our bodies do the talking. Both of us seem content with just lying on the beach, enjoying each other's company and this intimate moment. There's no rush, no need to move faster, only the perfect joy of two people exploring each other, of being able to express our feelings without the need for words.

I feel safe with him, cherished.

When we finally pull apart, we both lie supine, staring at the sky.

"Why is the distance measured in light years?" Christian asks.

"Most stars are too far away. The number in kilometers would be too big; it's impractical..."

"And why did you use kilometers to measure the distance to the sun instead of miles?"

"It's a convention to use the metric system so that all scientists around the world speak the same language. Different units of measurement can be a real pain for engineering students. I remember entire homework assignments dedicated to converting values from one system to the other."

"Can't you use a computer program or an app for that?"

"In real life, yes." I turn my head sideways to look at him, our eyes locking again. "But in a homework exercise, you have to show all the passages, so you gotta learn the traditional way."

"Fair enough." He smiles. "So what's the weirdest unit you had to work with?"

I think for a second. "Definitely the slug."

"The slug? There's a scientific unit called *slug*?"

"Yep."

"What does it measure?"

"Mass. It's the mass accelerated by one foot over square second when a force of one pound is exerted on it."

Christian keeps smiling. "And in human terms?"

"One slug weighs more or less 32.2 pounds."

"That's one fat snail."

"I guess," I say, laughing.

I want him to kiss me again. And something in my gaze must give my wish away because he rolls on top of me and presses his lips to mine.

Ah, the romantic power of the US Customary System.

I don't know how much time we spend wrapped in each other's arms, but I'm glad we're the only two people on this beach, as our conduct isn't 100 percent proper for a public space.

I'd stay here all night, but when the ocean breeze turns into a strong wind, we both begin to shiver. Even if we don't want to, we have to leave, unless we're looking to turn into popsicles.

Christian drives me back home and walks me to the door. We kiss again on the landing, but I'm not ready to invite him in, not *yet*. I like him, but I'm taking things slowly. I haven't dated anyone new in ten years and I have no idea what the rules are these days. But I know I won't jump into bed with a man on a first date—*or is this a second date? Does an afternoon together in a closet count?*

Either way, I'm not ready for the next step. I'm trying desperately to think of a polite way to convey all this without sounding as if I'm not interested when Christian surprises me by saying, "I have to go, early flight to catch tomorrow morning."

Perfect solution, really. Solves everything. So why am I immediately assaulted by doubts?

Doesn't he like me enough to want to come in?

"Oh, okay," I say.

He smiles. "Next time we go out, I'll make sure I don't have to be anywhere outside the city the next day."

First Date Theorem. Hypothesis: we're going out again. Conclusion: he likes me.

I blush. "That would be nice."

As a strong emotion crosses his features, his brows drop and his eyes widen. "I don't know what your ex was thinking," he says. "But I'm glad we met in that closet."

I can't stop a huge smile from spreading across my face. "Yeah, me too."

We kiss again, and when Christian leaves, I stand on my doorstep watching his car until it disappears around the corner.

Walking into my house, I touch two fingers to my lips... Maybe Winter was right. Maybe I really had forgotten how being in love was supposed to feel. My breath catches at that.

Don't be ridiculous, Lana, you can't be in love after one date.

Right. I can't.

Can I?

13

CHRISTIAN

"What's with the stupid grin, boss?" Penny asks me the next morning. We're in my home office at our usual stations: me behind the desk, and my assistant on the other side in her leather chair.

Telling Lana I had to be on a plane this morning was a white lie to spare her the embarrassment of not inviting me in. I could sense she wasn't ready and was struggling to find a polite way to turn me away.

Anyway, today, Penny is presenting me with various brands' proposals to hire me as a spokesperson.

Christian Slade, the new face of... yet to be determined.

"Nothing," I say, pursing my lips.

Penny, the nosiest assistant on Earth, doesn't fall for it. "So the mysterious picnic basket for two Jeff prepared last night was for some other smiley dude?"

"That man needs to learn how to keep his mouth shut."

"And you need to learn how to share more," Penny says. "I manage all aspects of your life, public *and* private. If you're dating someone I need to know who, when, where, for how long... what to tell the press, and what to keep confidential..."

Technically, she's right. But still...

"Oh, so yours is merely a professional interest..." I tease her.

Penny sighs, frustrated. "Do I have to beg? I'm dying here; you haven't dated anyone in a year. Who is this mystery woman?"

"Tell you what." I lean my elbows forward on my desk. "Wednesday night, I need a location for a cooking lesson, somewhere nice but private. Jeff will be the teacher. Find the right spot, and I'll tell you two horrible gossips everything."

When I first devised this plan, I thought of having the lesson here, but as per the flashy mansion problem, I ruled out the idea. And it has to be on Wednesday night because Lana told me she's free. But before asking her out again, I want to be sure the date can actually happen.

"You want to learn how to cook?" Penny raises a skeptical eyebrow. "Are you playing the chef in a movie I know nothing about?"

"The class wouldn't be strictly for one."

"So how many people would be involved?" She jots down a note on her agenda, the image of a professional assistant.

"Two students," I say with a grin.

Penny beams back. "All right, boss, I'll find you the best kitchen for hire in LA." She stands up. "In the meantime, review those proposals and let me know if you're interested in being the new face of something."

I watch her go and smile to myself. When Lana invited me to take a cooking class, my first reaction was to think, *There goes another normal thing couples do that we never could.* I tossed and turned in bed last night, trying to find a way to still make it happen. The idea of making the lesson private is so simple, I'm surprised it took me all night to figure it out. But now, learning to cook seems like the perfect opportunity for another undercover date.

Dates.

To learn our way around the kitchen, we're going to need more than one lesson. And if Penny finds the right location, we won't risk the paps—or anyone else—crashing in. Perfect to protect my secret.

Yeah, mate, but how long do you plan to keep your real identity hidden? a tiny voice whispers in my ear. *You're being dishonest.*

Technically, I haven't lied.

No, but eventually you must tell her.

True.

If I want to keep dating Lana, and I do, I won't be able to conceal my real life from her.

But is it so wrong to enjoy this newfound anonymity a little longer?

I haven't had a relationship untainted by my public persona since I was eighteen, and I'm so damn tired of interactions that reek of hidden agendas.

Lana is the first woman I've dated in years who I'm 100 percent sure is genuine, so I'm not ready to give up the authenticity of our connection. Not yet. Hopefully not ever.

Seems like I'm sporting a bad case of "like me for me" syndrome.

But that doesn't make it right to be shady with Lana, that same voice adds.

Today my conscience is hell-bent on calling me out.

"Okay, okay," I say out loud to the empty room. "I'll tell her."

When?

Soon, I promise myself.

Very soon.

* * *

"It's not fair," Penny protests on Wednesday evening. "Why does Jeff get to meet Lana and I don't?"

We're at home in the entrance hall; I'm about to leave to go pick up Lana, and I really don't have time for my assistant to throw a tantrum. But I listen to her anyway. I owe Penny. Without her help, tonight wouldn't be happening.

Penny found the perfect location to host a cooking course: a real restaurant available to rent on its closing night. A solution that delivers a professional kitchen, a place to eat afterward, total privacy, and saves me from showing Lana my house. And my assistant secured the spot at record speed so that I was able to call Lana two days after our first date to ask her out again. She said yes.

Unfortunately, getting all this set up meant disclosing that I'm dating someone not only to Penny, but to Jeff as well. And I had to explain to both of them that Lana has no idea who I am—publicly. Privately, Lana knows me better after one date and a couple of hours spent in a closet together one afternoon than most of my supposed friends here in Hollywood.

"Jeff's the teacher," I reply to Penny's objection. "Can't have a lesson without one."

"Why can't I come as a student?" my PA asks. "As your driver?"

"Three's already a crowd." I'm merciless. "And I can't have a driver; Lana thinks I'm a mid-list actor at best, remember? Or that I act in soap operas, or worse, that I'm that guy hopping jobs while I wait for my big break."

She snorts at that. "Yeah, right. It's still not fair."

A stab of guilt slashes at me. Penny really went out of her way to organize this date for me. She found the right space, rented it, typed and printed the class syllabus and recipe book, and delivered to the kitchen all the ingredients Jeff bought for tonight's demonstration. And I don't want to sound like an ungrateful bastard, but...

"Come on, you'll meet Lana soon. And I'm sure Jeff will give you a blow-by-blow of the night."

Jeff's enthusiasm about tonight has been so off the charts I almost regretted asking him—not that I had another choice. I just hope he's a decent actor and won't get us caught.

"It's not the same." Penny pouts.

"Sorry, but for now, you have to stick to Google stalking."

"I didn't stalk Lana on Google."

I arch a skeptical eyebrow at that.

"Okay, I might've looked her up once or twice. That's hardly stalking."

"If you really want to see her, you can drop Jeff off and wait in the car for us to arrive. But that's creepy."

"Totally creepy," Penny agrees. "I'm not doing that."

"Then you'll have to wait to meet Lana." I drop my hands on her shoulders. "But I want you to because it'd mean she's still going out with me and I like this woman."

Penny smiles at that. "You make me so proud," she says.

"You sound like my mother now."

"All right, kiddo." She smirks and wriggles away, pushing me toward the door. "Go have fun."

I grab the Tesla's key card and I'm out of the door. "I will."

14

LANA

As I get home on Wednesday night early enough to get ready for my second date with Christian, I meander through the boxes littering my hall and hop right into the shower.

When I re-emerge all scrubbed and with low blood pressure from the hot water, I sag onto the bed wrapped in a robe with a towel around my head and text Winter.

TO WINTER

Is the photography course confirmed for tomorrow?

FROM WINTER

Yep

Working on the program right now

TO WINTER

You're the best

Thanks so much again for pushing me to come

I'm super excited

FROM WINTER

You should be

Besides an awesome subject and teacher

70% of the students are males in their thirties

TO WINTER

Mmm, about that...

I'm already dating someone

FROM WINTER

What?

I mean W.H.A.T.?

I go away for a week and you turn your life around

TO WINTER

Yeah, that's the spirit

I'm dating someone new

I have a new friend

I'm learning to cook

And how to use a camera

Meet the new me

How was Hawaii BTW?

FROM WINTER

Fantastic

Best volcano shots of my career

Should I be jealous?

Of the new friend, not the date

And who are you dating?

CAMILLA ISLEY

Closet Man

My screen lights up with an incoming call the second my last message is marked as read.

"Hi," I pick up.

"Closet Man, huh?" Winter says in a sultry tone. "Do tell."

"He called last week and asked me on a date, and we're going out again tonight."

"I need specifics," Winter demands.

So I tell her about the ocean-side picnic and the cooking class Christian has invited me to tonight.

When he proposed it as our second date, I was surprised. On the beach, I had the impression he thought taking cooking lessons together would be lame, or that he wasn't interested at all. I never expected him to find a course and book a class for us less than a week later. And when I proposed we learned to cook together, I had meant to take the lessons online. Like a sort of home date where we would've cooked dinner together. But I was happy he booked a professional course, I only hope the enrollment fee wasn't too expensive.

"This guy sounds like a keeper," Winter says when I'm done.

"Oh, you know," I say vaguely. "It's only early days. I'm not sure I'm ready for something serious so soon after coming out of a ten-year relationship." I pause for a second, undecided if I want to ask the next question. "Have you... Have you seen her? Them?"

"No, sweetheart, I'm sorry. My sister is hiding from me as well. Bet she's too ashamed to show her face around these days."

When I accepted Winter's offer to move in with her, I'd wondered if I'd bump into Summer visiting her sister. Apparently not. I'm not sure if I'm more relieved or saddened by the thought.

I sigh. "No, of course. At least she isn't flaunting her relationship with Johnathan."

"Are you okay?" Winter's tone has turned serious.

"I am," I say sincerely. "But is it weird I still miss Summer, but not Johnathan?"

"We were in your life way before he was. We've known each other forever... But, Lana, if you want to forgive Summer, it's your choice, no one will judge you either way. You don't have to be tough on principle. Do what's best for yourself, and yourself alone."

"I want to forgive your sister, I really do." I bite my lower lip. "Maybe not right now, I'm not ready yet... but eventually. Even if she hasn't asked to be forgiven or said she's sorry."

"I can't believe we came from the same womb."

"Same egg," I correct her. "You're identical twins."

"Please don't remind me. Why couldn't I share most of my DNA with you instead?"

"My cells aren't artistic enough for you."

"At least they're not evil. But really, about Summer... If you're only waiting for her to apologize, I can nudge her. She's probably gone into hiding because she's too scared to face you. But if I were to tell her you're open to a reconciliation..."

"No, I still need time. But even if the wound eventually heals, the scar will always be there. Say I forgive Summer, how could I ever trust her again? And what's a friendship without trust? She broke that bond between us, and it will never be like it was before..."

"I know, and it makes me so mad I want to bitch-slap my sister so bad. I really don't understand what possessed her."

"Neither do I." I sigh into the phone.

"Any news on the work front?"

"Nope. I've sent out several inquiries, but so far I've only gotten a bunch of rejections and some lukewarm requests for more information. But I'm sure everything will pan out eventually."

"Sorry, I didn't mean to upset you."

"No, it's okay. I've come to terms with this new reality and I'm trying to fix it."

"Still, I don't want to get you in a wistful mood before your date," Winter says. "Let's talk about the important stuff... What are you wearing tonight?"

"I was thinking something understated, like jeans and a simple T-shirt. I don't know what's on the menu, but we'll probably have to get our hands dirty in the kitchen?"

"In the kitchen only? What underwear are you wearing?"

"What kind of question is that?"

"The kind that lets me know if you're going to wear granny panties no one is supposed to ever see, or sexy underwear that begs to be uncovered."

"I'm wearing the latter," I reply, smiling like an idiot. "Just in case."

"Good," Winter says, her voice full of glee. "Go have fun with your tall, British stranger. And take notes, I expect a full report tomorrow."

We hang up and I go to the underwear drawer, dragging my fingers over the folded undies. Pink lace or black?

15

CHRISTIAN

Lana hops down the steps of her house wearing a golden-yellow T-shirt, jeans, and white sneakers. Her hair is tied high up in a ponytail. If I thought she was sexy in a dress, this girl-next-door style is a total knock out.

"Hey." She beams, hugging me, sapphire eyes alight in the late afternoon sun.

I'd like to keep her in my arms forever, but the urgency of getting back into the car before someone recognizes me is more pressing. So I let go, give her a quick peck on the lips, and open the passenger door for her.

Once we've pulled away, Lana asks, "Do you know what we're going to cook tonight?"

"Err, no. I booked a beginner class but didn't ask for the specifics. Any preferences?"

"No, not really. I'm a good fork, I can eat almost anything."

"Yeah?" I tap the wheel.

"Yep, but I draw the line at crispy insects."

"You know many people who regularly eat bugs?"

"There's a huge environmentally conscious movement that

advocates for cricket flour and such, but that's too green even for me." Lana shifts in the passenger seat and adjusts her seat belt. "I try to walk everywhere and don't use a drier, to limit my carbon footprint, but crickets in my food? Sorry, can't get past that."

She really cracks me up.

"I'm confident crickets won't be on the menu tonight," I say.

At least, I hope not. Otherwise, I'll have to find a new cook, 'cause mine will be dead.

* * *

The restaurant's kitchen is a medium-sized room crammed with stainless-steel appliances, pots, frying pans, and obscure cooking tools.

On a shiny steel counter, an orderly row of ingredients is already set: vegetables, ground meat, tomato sauce, cheeses, pasta, eggs, and flour—hopefully not crickets.

"Ah, Christian." Jeff does a grand show of meeting me for the first time as he extends his hand. "We spoke on the phone; nice to meet you in person."

"Jeff." I shake his hand. "This is Lana."

"How wonderful to meet you," Jeff says, a bit too eagerly.

I hope Lana takes him for an over-enthusiastic teacher.

She must, because she gives him one of her big smiles and shakes his hand, not a hint of suspicion on her face.

"Welcome to our beginners cooking course," Jeff intones. "Our approach will be a learn-by-doing system that I prefer to lengthy explanations. So... here." Jeff hands out aprons. "Who's ready to get their hands dirty?"

"Aren't we waiting for the other students?" Lana asks.

"No, dear." Jeff shakes his head. "This is our special *a deux* lesson plan."

Lana turns to me. "You booked a chef only for us?"

I nod. "I thought it'd be more intimate."

She makes an unreadable face as if she's split between being impressed and being worried. "Let me know how much the fee was; I'll Venmo you the money."

Such a simple but significant offer. I'm so used to being surrounded by freeloaders that Lana's words bear more weight than they would with a regular person.

"Don't worry," I say.

"But—"

"Err, should we begin?" Jeff interrupts her protest.

Lana throws me a we'll-settle-this-later stare, before turning to him and saying, "Sure."

"Fantastic." Jeff smiles as he announces the program for tonight. "For our first lesson, I wanted to start with something not too challenging, so I thought we should tackle some easier family favorites."

Oh, he's so loving this. I wonder if Jeff's secret calling is to teach cooking, rather than being my private chef.

"But to avoid making the class too boring," he continues, "I've selected three separate courses: an American classic—homemade mac and cheese—a more elaborate ragù, and a risotto. Lots to do; we should get started."

Lana smiles at me as she ties on her apron. "Yum, I'm already hungry," she says. "Do we get to eat what we make afterward?"

"I think so." I look at Jeff for confirmation.

"A table has been set for you in the main restaurant," he says. "We wouldn't want any food to go to waste. Are we ready to start?"

We both nod, and Jeff launches into his explanation. "Since the ragù takes longer, we'll start with that. Browned vegetables are at the base of every great ragù. A simple mix of carrots, celery, and for a more tasteful sauce, shallots instead of onions."

I turn to Lana. "It only remains to decide who has to peel the onions."

"Shallots," Jeff corrects me. "And you only need to remove the outer layer; the veggie chopper will do the rest." He points to a mini blender. "Please follow the recipe on page one of the course cookbook. There, you'll find all the recipes for tonight's class so you can try them again at home."

Lana grabs a carrot and a peeler and turns to me with a mischievous grin. "Last to peel the carrots does the dishes."

* * *

Damn, making food from scratch is hard work. But also fun, especially with Lana as my cooking partner. Plus, Jeff is a wonderful teacher.

For two and a half hours we slaved over the stove, and now it's time to enjoy the final product. In the main restaurant's room, a table for two has been set for us. So, with Jeff's help, we bring our plates and sit to have dinner.

"Very well," Jeff says. "I suggest eating the saffron risotto first, as it's the most delicate dish, then the mac and cheese, and finally the ragù. I've also selected a beautiful red from Napa that goes nicely with all three dishes. Enjoy."

He withdraws back to the kitchen, leaving us to savor the food we made—except for the homemade fettuccine. Jeff showed off making them from scratch to go with the ragù. In ten minutes, he mixed eggs, flour, and water, kneaded them together, rolled the dough into a thin sheet, and cut the fettuccine with a knife. The cutting was so quick and even that both Lana and I thought it was a magic trick. But tasting the final result, there's no doubt the pasta is real.

"Mmm," Lana moans after eating a forkful of risotto.

"Cheers to the chef." I raise my glass to her.

"Cheers." Lana clinks her glass against mine. "Jeff is amazing. I'm sure if I tried to cook this on my own, the risotto would turn out a disaster. I wish I could have him cooking at my house every day."

The last statement comes out in a "what an impossible thing to wish for" tone that throws me off. Because having a private chef is one of the many things I take for granted.

Should I tell her now?

I'm aware that the more I wait, the harder it'll be to explain everything I've kept from her. But I also don't want to ruin the best second date ever by dropping the did-I-mention-I'm-kind-of-famous bomb mid-dinner.

"Yeah, right?" I laugh it off, uncomfortable.

"Did I say something wrong?"

"No, nothing you said. It's about me."

"What about you?" Lana asks.

Perfect second date or not, I have to fess up. Lana is a good person and has had enough lies spun to her already.

"I—" *How do I tell her without sounding totally mental?* "I haven't been completely honest with you about my life."

"Mm, yeah," she says, surprising me. "I've noticed you get a little standoffish whenever I ask a personal question. I thought it was a British thing."

"It's not."

"So, what is it?" Lana sits up straighter, on the alert, a crease of worry crossing her forehead. "Are you secretly married, engaged, seeing someone else?" Her eyes flick to my left hand and back up.

"No, nothing like that," I hurry to reassure her. "It's about my job."

"Oh." Her back relaxes. "Is it about the secret movie?"

"In part, yes."

"Is it something criminal?" she asks, her tone light again. "Are you with the Mob, secretly laundering money through a sketchy production?"

"No." I can't help but laugh. "Nothing illegal, I swear."

"But it's something that makes you uncomfortable, right?"

"Yeah, in a way, yes."

"Then you don't have to tell me. Not right now, anyway," she says, and goes back to eating her pasta with gusto.

Lana has no idea what she's agreeing to stay in the dark about.

Indecision must show on my face because she reaches her hand across the table to place it on top of mine. "Hey, I don't mind waiting, really. I haven't told you every little thing about myself, either. We can take things slow. Okay?"

Lana sounds so reassuring, and the temptation to wait is so big, I let myself believe it's okay not to come clean tonight.

Without the weight of my secret hanging over me, dinner becomes even more fantastic. I can be myself with Lana, no need to keep my guard up, no preconceptions, and no fear of being used.

Just us.

* * *

On the way back to her house, Lana is quieter in the car, but at the same time, she's... *more.* She keeps her gaze trained out the window but reaches for my hand where it sits on the armrest between us, curling her fingers into mine. Streetlights dart past us one by one and, in their fleeting light, whenever I dare take my eyes off the road for a short peek, I notice a slight blush on her cheeks.

What is she thinking? Does this mean I get invited in tonight?

"Here we are." I pull up in front of her house and, shifting the car into park, I turn to face her.

Her I-have-secrets smile makes an appearance. "Any early flights to catch tomorrow morning?" she asks, eyes sparkling even in the dark.

"No," I say, the sound cut off in my throat.

"Nightcap?"

"I'd love one," I say, and again I can't keep my voice from going a little husky.

When we get out of the car, it's late enough I don't have to worry about indiscreet eyes, so I leave my baseball cap in the car and follow her to the front door.

Lana lets us in, and I wonder how this is going to work. Are we going to pretend I really did just come in for coffee? *Did* I just come in for coffee? She's a mystery, and I love it.

Lana closes the door behind us and leans against it without turning on the lights. She smiles at me again in the semi-darkness, her mouth as inviting as sin. I go to her, loving the delicate curve of her neck as she inches her chin up to meet my lips.

So I guess coffee isn't on anyone's mind.

Good.

We kiss and tumble through the house, stumbling our feet on unclosed boxes that litter the way to her bedroom. Clothes fall off on the way. We're both shirtless when we reach the bed and find it already occupied by the cats.

"Sorry," Lana says. "I'll get rid of them."

The view of her grabbing one cat under each arm and dragging them out of the room would be comic, if not for the distracting pink lace of her bra that's preventing me from swallowing.

When she returns, she shuts the door firmly behind herself as she says, "Dropped them on the couch. I hope they won't mind sleeping there for a night."

I can tell the pause has made her shy. So I slow down. I pull her to me, pressing my lips on her neck, just below her ear. "I'm sure they'll be fine." My mouth leaves a trail of kisses all the way to her collarbone.

I take my time kissing all her hesitations away until Lana gets bold again and her hands land squarely on my chest as she pushes me backward onto the covers...

* * *

The next morning, I wake up with a sneeze, my nose itchy. I push up onto my elbows to find a cat's tail tickling my chin.

Didn't we shut the little buggers out last night?

The thought triggers much more pleasant memories of the end of my date with Lana, which makes sleeping with a feline ass so close to my face an acceptable price to pay.

Lana stirs next to me, without waking up. Careful not to disturb her, I grab my phone, lower the screen brightness to the darker setting, and text Penelope.

TO PENNY

Need help

FROM PENNY

It's 5 AM

I get her reply plus a sleepy emoji.

TO PENNY

Please

I need you to bring breakfast

FROM PENNY
Where?

TO PENNY
To Lana's

The emoji of a cat with hearts in place of eyes appears on my screen, followed by a question:

FROM PENNY
You spent the night?

TO PENNY
Obviously

FROM PENNY
What does my boy want for breakfast?

TO PENNY
Coffee and croissants

I'll text you the address

FROM PENNY
On it, boss

PS. I forgive you for the early hour, but only in the name of love

Forty-five minutes later, I get another text from Penny saying she's here. I tell her to come up the walkway, and I sneak out of bed to meet her at the door. I open it a fraction and peer outside, not wanting to get out of the house where anyone could spot me. Penny is patiently waiting on the landing with sleepy-but-smug eyes, holding a carton tray with two coffee cups and a paper bag.

"Morning." She smirks. "Had a good night of *sleep*?" Her tone is saucier than I like.

I take the tray and bag from her. "You're the best and, no, we're not talking about it now."

Penny winks at me in a later-then way, chirps "Enjoy!" and waves goodbye. With a few hopping steps, she's back in her car and speeding down the empty street.

I sneak back into bed, drop the tray onto the nightstand, and wake Lana with a kiss on the forehead. She stretches her arms and those wonderful sapphire eyes blink open.

The moment we make eye contact, a delightful blush spreads on her cheeks.

"Morning," I say.

"Morning." She self-consciously wraps the sheets around herself and sits up.

"I went to get breakfast."

White lie, I know.

I hand her a paper cup and a pastry.

Lana takes a bite and, with her mouth half full, she moans, "Mm, delicious. Thank you." She stares out the window at the backyard still coated in semi-darkness. "What time is it?"

"Nearly six. Sorry, I have a meeting in a few hours and I need to go home, shower, and get changed first." Another lie. I simply want to leave Lana's place before there are too many people around. "But I wanted to have breakfast with you." This, at least, is true.

"That's..." She blushes again. "Sweet of you."

We eat the rest of the croissants in near silence, the only conversation happening with stolen stares.

When Lana is done, I use a napkin to clean her fingers and steal one last kiss.

"I should go," I say.

"Thank you for breakfast," Lana says, and then, with another, deeper blush, she adds, "But next time I want to spend all morning in bed with you."

"Deal." I grin like a fool. "But can we please leave the cats out?"

Two sets of yellow eyes fix me in a silent challenge.

"Sorry," Lana says. "I let them sleep with me now, and they don't give up privileges easily."

"But didn't we shut them out yesterday?"

"Yes, but they know how to open the door."

"Then they really are your cats."

"Why?"

"Because they're super smart." I kiss the tip of her nose. "I'll call you later, all right?"

"Yeah."

She makes to get up, but I nudge her back down. "Stay. I can let myself out."

We kiss again and, regretfully, I leave Lana's bedroom.

Before exiting, I check the street outside. No one's there. I quickly hop down the steps and take refuge in the Tesla.

No one saw me.

Mission Incognito Morning After accomplished.

16

LANA

After Christian leaves, I snuggle back under the covers. Flashes of last night make it impossible for me to wipe a silly, sated grin from my lips.

Basking in the still-vivid memories, I close my eyes and relive small moments of Christian in bed: the way the fabric of his T-shirt pulled tight across his chest as he removed it. How the curves of his biceps flexed when he was above me. The adorable way his soft blond hair fell forward, curling over his forehead. Or how sweetly disheveled he looked this morning as he brought me breakfast in bed.

I try to commit to memory all the lines of his body... a work of art.

I can count the men I've slept with on one hand, so I'm not a grand expert in male anatomy. But I'm sure bodies like Christian's are not that common. He's a sculpture of chiseled muscle with skin as smooth as marble.

Over an image of his perfect stomach, I doze off again, cocooned in total bliss, until my alarm goes off an hour later. Since I don't have to make breakfast, I snooze it twice and enjoy the excitement mixed with the tiredness a night spent making love has left me with.

When I can delay no longer, I get up, waltzing through the house as I wash up, get dressed, and feed the cats.

They're still indignant that I tried to force them out of the bedroom last night; funny how quickly sleeping in my bed became an entitlement. So I trick Cengel and Boles into purring by giving them one of their favorite wet food treats—a New Zealand mackerel and lamb mix. I should probably start weaning them down to less expensive cat food. But since doom hasn't stricken yet, I want them to enjoy their favorite meals while I can afford to provide them.

Peace made, I grab my purse and laptop messenger bag and leave the house.

I'm ready to make the usual uneventful walk to work, but the moment I set foot on the front steps, I'm assaulted by what must be a thousand camera flashes all going off at once. The curb in front of my house is crowded with a dozen or more people —*photographers*, as they're each holding a big black camera in their hands.

"Miss Voynich!" one screams. *They know my name?* "How long have you been Christian Slade's girlfriend?"

"Are you officially a couple?" another echoes.

Each man shouts a different question.

"How did you meet?"

"Are you getting married?"

"Are you pregnant?"

"What?" I shout to be heard over the noise. "What are you talking about? You have the wrong person."

"Are you denying you're dating Christian?"

"No," I say as I try to push through the crowd to get on my way to work. "But why do you care?"

"Is that an official statement?" someone to my left asks.

"Are you on the record, Miss Voynich?" another one shouts from the back.

"No, I'm not on any record." *What are they even talking about? I don't care; I just want to get past this mob.* "Please, let me pass."

But they don't budge and keep on asking questions.

"You have the wrong person," I repeat, my frustration starting to show. "*Please* leave me alone."

"Are you claiming Christian Slade didn't spend the night here?" another guy insists.

Were these people following us? Why?

"That's none of your business."

"So is it true?" the same guy insists.

I'm still trying to push my way through, but the throng is too thick. Too many bodies pressing in on me. I'm beginning to panic when someone gently grabs me by the arm.

"Come with me, Miss Voynich." It's a young woman with light brown skin, striking turquoise eyes, and a halo of black curls. "I work for Christian; he sent me to help you get out of this mess."

"Christian knows about this?" I ask.

"Yes, and he's sorry. He didn't want this to happen, but I'm here to help."

"What *is* happening? Why send you? Why couldn't he come himself?"

"The paparazzi are blocking the entrance to his house, too. He couldn't come."

"Paparazzi? I don't understand."

"I'll explain everything in the car." She nudges me toward the side of the road. "Now, please come with me. I'll drive you to work."

For lack of better alternatives, I follow this stranger who seems to know me and, more to the point, how to handle a swarm of frenzied paparazzi.

Like a pro, she elbows a passage for us through the crowd, shoving the photographers away while repeating, "Show's over. Clear the way. Now be good boys and let us pass, or you're never going to get another piece of Christian ever again, and that's a promise."

Like magic, the sea of people parts, opening a narrow corridor for us. As we walk past, the photographers keep shouting questions, only directing them at my companion now. They seem to know each other.

"Penny, does Christian have an official statement?"

"Are you on the record?"

"Are he and Lana in a relationship?"

"Guys!" the woman, Penny, shouts. "Christian's position is not to comment at this time."

"Oh, come on, give us something," a younger guy pleads.

"I *said* no comment."

One last step and we reach the woman's car. No, not her car, but Christian's red Tesla. She opens the passenger door for me and shuts it behind me. I buckle in as the photographers, unperturbed, keep shooting pictures of me through the car window. The flashes only stop when the woman gets in the driver's seat and we pull away, leaving the flock of paparazzi behind us.

"Sorry," she says. "I haven't officially introduced myself. I'm Penelope Jones, Christian's personal assistant."

I'm too confused to even say anything, so I let her do the talking.

"This whole situation must seem strange to you, but I can explain everything, and Christian will call you later. If you still want to talk to him."

I turn to her expectantly, and she launches into her explanation. "Christian is an actor."

"I knew that already."

"Not like how everyone in LA is an '*actor*'." If she had her hands free, she'd be making air quotes. "He's the real deal. Christian is famous. A celebrity."

This all sounds so ridiculous; I have no idea how to respond.

"He didn't tell you he was so successful because you're the first person in years who's not after him for his status or his money. But he'll explain everything to you later when you talk. Now, he sent me to make sure you were okay, and that you made it to work on time."

My head is ringing with new information. *Christian, a famous actor? A celebrity?*

"What we think happened here," Penelope continues, "is that someone must've spotted him coming out of your house this morning and called the press. Or maybe the paparazzi had been stalking him since last night. There's really no way to know. The point is, you're busted now. I'm afraid we won't be able to get the press off your back entirely. We're going to try to manage them as well as we can from our end, but there could always be some scumbag following you around." She looks in the rearview mirror. "It's already a good sign no one's tailing us."

I make a mental note to add "crazy paparazzi are not chasing our car" to the positive aspects of my day.

"Anyway, the press shouldn't be allowed on campus," Penelope adds in a brisk, professional tone. "So at least they should leave you alone at work. But the curb in front of your house is a public space, so if some rogue paparazzi decides to stalk you there, there's not much we can do about it."

The words "rogue paparazzi" are so out of my frame of reference that I remain stunned into silence. The concept belongs in a parallel universe, not my quiet life.

We arrive on campus, and Christian's assistant parks the car in a drop-off spot.

"Is this entrance okay?" Penelope asks.

"Yes," I manage, still too overwhelmed to articulate more.

"I know it's a lot to take in, but I promise the paps aren't too bad once you get used to them. Unfortunately, they're par for the course when you're around Chris."

And then it hits me: I've been dating a superstar and had no idea. How? True, I never watch TV, but am I really so out of tune? It's something Johnathan always accused me of, that I live too much in the clouds, and apparently, he was right.

"This is my card." She hands me a crisp white rectangle. "If you have any problem at all, call me. I can handle almost any situation."

I take the card from her. "Thank you."

I want to ask a million questions, but not to her. Only Christian can give me the answers I seek.

How mad should I be at him?

I count to ten.

Right, Lana. Better to hear his side of the story before I jump to any conclusions.

"What time do you get off today?" Penelope asks.

"My last lecture of the day finishes at five," I say.

"Christian has asked me to pick you up again. I can take you back to your place, or to his house to..." For the first time since we met, her speech falters. "...talk things through, you know? So does five work?"

I should say no. Once the lecture is over, I should go right back to the lab and work on my research.

"Do I have to decide now?"

"No, later is fine. Just shoot me a text whenever you've made a decision. Sound good?"

"Yeah, thank you."

Still in a haze, I get out of the car and walk the familiar paths to the Engineering Department. Inside the building, the familiarity of the halls and the no-paparazzi-allowed policy are comforting.

Since I didn't walk to work, I have half an hour to spare before my first lecture. With no previous scheduled classes, the auditorium is empty, meaning I'm free to sit at the teacher's desk and power up my laptop for a quick stalk.

I google Christian Slade and stare, dumbstruck, at the number of hits.

About 135,000,000 results (0.49 seconds)

The top search result is a Wikipedia page, followed by an IMDb profile. As for the little row of image results, it's a string of pictures all featuring him on the cover of a magazine in different macho poses.

Different poses, same headline: Sexiest Man Alive.

Lower on the page, there's everything from videos and interviews to movie trailers and gossip columns about his love life. I scroll down till the end of the webpage and note the news articles about his past relationships.

Wow, he's sure been busy dating a lot of beautiful women.

I don't recognize any of them, but they all seem to be celebrities.

I open a new tab and google Isaac Newton, to get perspective.

About 68,000,000 results (0.48 seconds)

So, apparently, my boyfriend is twice as famous as the man who discovered gravity.

But is Christian even my boyfriend?

I thought last night was the beginning of something, but what is a Hollywood megastar doing with me?

I'm so confused. I need a second opinion.

So I call Winter.

"Hello-aww," she picks up on the third ring with half a yawn.

"Sorry, did I wake you?"

"Mm-hm, but it doesn't matter," she says, still sounding groggy. "I should get up anyway. What's up?"

"Do you know who Christian Slade is?"

"Yeah, sure. Everyone knows. You'd have to live under a rock not to know."

"Well, I didn't know!"

"Okay, fine, honey," Winter says in a yoga-teacher tone. "Why are we talking about Christian Slade first thing in the morning, anyway?"

"He's Closet Man."

"Wait, what?" Now she sounds alert.

"Turns out my struggling actor wasn't quite as struggling as I thought."

"Whoa. I mean, wow! How... I don't know what to say."

"Me neither. I woke up this morning and my house was surrounded by paparazzi. At first, I thought they had the wrong person, but then this woman, *his personal assistant*, showed up to escort me to work, saying Christian couldn't come himself as his house, too, was swamped by the press. I mean, can you believe this?"

"No, it's so... so... How?"

"How could I not know?"

"Yeah. I mean, when the dude told you he was an actor, you

didn't look him up?"

I flare my nostrils. "Winter, how many years have we been living in LA?"

"Ten?" I can picture her scrunching her face to do the math. "Why?"

"And how many men have you met in that time who've told you they were actors?"

"Okay, I get your point!"

"Did you google all of them?"

"No, fair enough."

Point made, I move on to the pressing issue. "So, what do I do now?"

"Well, you kissed Christian Slade, so, kudos to you, girl. If the sexiest man alive was interested in kissing me, I'd let him have his wicked way for as long as he wanted."

I bite my lower lip as I say, "Actually, we did a bit more than kissing. He spent the night. His assistant said someone must've seen him leave this morning and called the press."

"Hell, Lana. You had sex with him? You saw *the* Christian Slade naked?"

"Last time I checked, that's the only way to do certain things."

"Sorry, it's too much to wrap my head around. So you didn't recognize him, and he never told you? Not even a hint? How did he pull it off? Where did you guys go for your dates?"

"I've been thinking in the same loop nonstop since I got here. Listen, I don't have time to dissect everything now, but are you free for lunch?"

"Yeah. I have an appointment in Rancho Park at ten; I can drive up to you when I'm done."

"Perfect. Text me when you're here. I finish my morning lecture at eleven thirty. I can do an early lunch."

"All right, I'll see you later."

"Later."

I hang up and still have enough time to click on one video before class.

It's a clip from a movie, a romantic scene.

There's a beautiful, super-attractive blonde standing outside a motel. Christian comes up from behind, and the woman, without turning, says, "Laurie, don't."

"Why not?" Christian asks, looking all serious and angsty.

"Because we can't," the blonde says, turning. "Because it's wrong. Because it would be so hard."

The camera now does a close-up of Christian's face. His expression changes from tormented to that mischievous, playful pout I like so much before he delivers the cheesiest line ever: "Nothing worthwhile has ever been easy."

That seems to do it for the woman because she launches herself into his arms and they make out against a column as the background music reaches its crescendo and the actress's hair twists in the wind in an epic, romantic moment that's so constructed I could gag.

The video ends, the screen freezing on a static thumbnail of the kiss airbrushed with fairy lights and the title of the movie written in bold characters at the bottom.

I stare at the image a little longer, and something churns in my gut. I wonder if recognizing so much of him in a movie scene is more cute or creepy. And I'm not sure what the proper reaction should be to seeing the man I'm dating pretend-kiss another woman on camera. But it's making me long for Christian to kiss me again. I want those lips pressed on mine.

As do half the women on the planet, apparently.

The video is a little shy of ten million views and has over twenty-two thousand comments.

I read a few.

Tanja Kaplan, 1 year ago:
I'm not gonna lie, this is one of my absolute favorite movie kisses.
There's something about it, they did it just right.
2.1k Likes, 25 Comments

Ceyda, 2 months ago (edited):
When he said "why not...." the emotion in his voice 🖤🖤🖤
764 Likes, 14 Comments

Sofia Murphy, 5 months ago:
Christian is so hot I can never stop loving him :-*
418 Likes, 5 Comments

Then it's mostly a series of CHRISTIAN SLADE I LOVE YOU,
CHRISTIAN MARRY ME messages all shouted out in capital
letters.

The man sure has some dedicated fans.

My head begins to spin again. Looks like tens of thousands of
women around the world are in love with him, or at least with the
idea of him.

And it's like a "you've got competition!" alert goes off in my
brain.

I don't give myself space to dwell on the realization. It's time for
my thermofluid dynamics class, and I owe it to my students to be
100 percent focused on delivering the best lesson I can. Hell knows
I've already been distracted enough lately. Any thought of the
sexiest man alive will have to wait.

17

LANA

"I swear I never went so deep into a Google Search rabbit hole," I tell Winter as we sit to eat salads at a table outside the food court.

"And what's your conclusion?" she asks, removing a plastic fork from its wrapper.

I take out my set of metallic, reusable, non-polluting cutlery, and say, "I'm overwhelmed, and I still have no idea what to do, or what this means for us." I stab a piece of feta cheese. "Do you think it's possible to have a normal relationship with a man so famous?"

"Normal, probably not," my friend says in a sage voice. "But extraordinary, why not?"

"I don't know... Aren't celebrities supposed to all get married between themselves?"

"No, plenty of actors marry civilians."

"Really?"

"Yeah." Winter nods as she picks out the olives and sets them to the side. "Matt Damon married a woman he met in a bar, right?"

"Who's Matt Damon?"

Winter rolls her eyes, exasperated. "You're hopeless, you know that?"

"I don't watch TV." I shrug and dig my fork into the salad.

"Well, gotta start now."

"Be honest. You seriously think I could fit into that world? I'm *so* not Hollywood."

"So? I can't pretend to know what dating one of the most famous actors in the world entails, because I have no clue. But whatever the hassle, is Christian being famous enough for you to not want to pursue the relationship?" Winter adds more dressing to her salad. "How far along are you with the man, feelings-wise?"

"This morning I would've told you that I haven't felt so alive in years and that everything seemed possible." I reach across and steal one of her discarded olives. "I was so happy, and I hate that I'm only filled with doubts now."

"Are you mad he didn't tell you?"

"Christian tried to tell me last night... before..."

"You two got naked?"

"Yep."

"Please explain: how does someone try and fail to tell the truth?"

"He told me he hadn't been completely honest with me about his life—his job, more specifically." I shove the last forkful of spinach into my mouth and sort the trash according to recycle bins. "And I said it was okay to wait, that he could tell me whenever he was ready."

"Weren't you curious?"

"More prejudiced," I admit. "I thought Christian wanted to confess he'd lied about acting for a living. I expected him to say his real job was at an accounting firm or something, not that he was *the* most famous actor on the planet."

"Darling, no one with that face would work at an accounting firm."

"Right? I feel like an idiot. How could I be so naïve?"

"Don't blame yourself." Winter reaches across the table to squeeze my hand. "Mr. Sexiest Man Alive should've told you."

"I'm withholding judgment on that until I hear what he has to say."

"So what's the real problem here?" Winter asks, reading between the lines.

I twist my fingers in my lap. "After what happened with Johnathan, I feel like I'm being blindsided again. I'm not even sure I'm ready to risk my heart on someone else, and Christian is the kind of man who makes women fall hard and fast..."

Winter snorts in agreement.

"I was already scared of how he made me feel before," I continue. "And now this... I'm afraid it's all going to be too much. That I'll end up in a far worse place than crying in a closet this time. I'm terrified of the kind of heartbreak you don't recover from. Remember when we talked about chest pains?"

"Sure."

"Christian is not someone you leave without having palpitations."

"Honey, I'm sorry to tell you, but there's no other kind of relationship worth risking your heart on. And even if you called it off now, judging from the shining light in your eyes, it could already be too late. Are you in love with the guy?"

A wave of heat warms my cheeks. "Don't be absurd. Way too soon for that."

"Mm..." She eyes me skeptically.

"I'm serious. I swear I'm not in love with him."

"Yet," she insists.

"Yet," I concede.

Winter wipes her mouth on a napkin and, with a mischievous grin, asks, "So, how was making love to him? As great as it looks on screen?"

I can't help the smile that spreads on my lips. "Emotionally, it was as intense as being sixteen and losing my virginity, but without the inexperience and awkward fumbling. He... he's great in bed." I blush again.

"Look at you, all sexed up! Sounds even better than in the movies."

"Now you get why I'm so scared?"

"I do, sweetheart, I really do. But you're the most determined, courageous person I know. You can't let fear dictate your actions. It's no way to live."

"Courageous? I'm not brave at all."

"No? You're kicking ass in a field that's dominated by testosterone."

"More I'm being kicked around," I say, thinking of my precarious position.

"Okay, how about this, then?" Winter leans back in her chair. "Every weekend you venture into the most dangerous neighborhoods of the city to tutor kids who don't have access to a fancy education, and don't tell me you don't risk at least being mugged every time you go there."

I open my mouth to protest, but I can't deny what she said is true. "Okay, maybe I don't have a problem walking through a dark alley at night, but you know I'm an introvert. People are scary. And is it so wrong for me to wish Christian was a regular, un-famous guy?"

Winter laughs at that.

"What?" I say.

"Most women dream of dating a movie star, and he had to go find the one woman who'd rather he be a nobody."

"Not a nobody; just someone who doesn't have millions of women fantasizing about him, that's all."

Winter's smile turns evil now.

"What's going on in that sadistic mind of yours?" I ask.

"Oh, I can't wait to see my sister's face when she learns you've rebounded with Christian Slade."

"Why? She likes him?"

"Dragged me to most of his movies..."

And as low and vindictive as it might sound, the revelation gives me a little, vengeful twinge of satisfaction. "Imagine when she finds out I would've never met Christian if I hadn't followed her and Johnathan to their hotel rendezvous."

"Even better." Winter keeps grinning and raises her cup. "Cheers!"

I clink my refillable bottle against her cup, and ask, "What are we toasting to?"

"To karma, the biggest bitch ever..."

As the end of my afternoon lecture draws near, I confess my professionalism slips a bit. I caved before class started and texted Penelope to please pick me up at five. With my future being so uncertain, it's irresponsible of me to leave this early, to not even check in at the lab. But my brain isn't in it. All I can think about is Christian and what he will have to say. Even if I spent three hours in the lab, flow-field imaging would be the furthest thing from my mind.

Still, since I'm stuck here until five, I do my best to focus on the lecture I'm giving but that doesn't stop me from checking the classroom clock every other minute. Already, convective heat transfer theory isn't my favorite subject to teach. And conservation equations are such a bore; it's hard to stay focused when all my brain wants to do is to skip ahead and decide on an action plan.

Should I ask Penelope to take me home, or drive me to Christian's place?

Normally I'd be nervous to see him for the first time after we spent the night together, but add everything else into the mix, and my anxiety has spiked. But the face-to-face has to happen at some point, right? And regardless of the complications, I want to see Christian, kiss him, and do... other stuff with him... and I need... clarifications.

At ten to five, I've finished my explanation of the enthalpy equation, and it'd be silly to start with the temperature equation when there's no way I could finish in time. So, to the joy of both me and my students, I dismiss class ten minutes early and brace myself for what's coming.

I walk out of the Engineering Department and across campus. When I reach the parking lot, Penelope is already waiting in the same spot where she dropped me off earlier. I wave at her and slide into the Tesla.

"Hello, Miss Voynich," she greets me as soon as I'm settled. "Did you have a nice day? Any trouble?"

"Not a peep from the press, thank you, and please call me Lana."

"Okay, Lana, where should I take you? Home, or to Christian's?"

"Does he want to see me?"

"Oh, he's dying to."

I fasten my seat belt. "But why didn't he call?"

"The boss wanted to give you space."

"Okay, then, I'd like to go to his place."

"Perfect." Penelope starts the engine and we pull away.

She drives through the Northern exit, then merges onto Sunset Boulevard to head northwest toward Beverly Hills.

Where does Christian even live? A mansion? That's where movie stars usually live, isn't it?

I get my answer as we keep driving northwest until we enter Trousdale Estates. We drive past rows of fenced-off mansions, their ultra-modern roofs barely visible behind the high hedges.

The gate we stop in front of isn't much different from the others we cruised past: solid, dark gray metal with twin security cameras atop and an access keypad column. Penelope lowers the window and enters a code to let us in.

"No press," I note aloud as we wait for the heavy-looking gate to slowly open.

"Yeah, we managed to clear them out by mid-morning," Penelope informs me. "And I checked your place, too, before coming to pick you up. It was clear as well."

"Thank you."

"No worries, it's my job."

I can't help but ask, "Do you often have to check for rogue paparazzi near the houses of Christian's girlfriends?"

"No." She smiles in a *busted* sort of way. "They usually have their own version of me to take care of that."

Right, because guys like Christian don't date women like me.

The gate finally opens and we slip inside, where a guard in a black uniform greets Penelope.

"Hi, Penny."

"Andy."

"Do I have to log your guest in?" the guard asks.

"No, the boss is expecting us."

"Go right ahead, then."

Penelope nods. We continue up the driveway to the house, and I do my best to prevent my jaw from dropping.

Christian's modern designer house sits on a terraced lot with a view of the city below. It's as white, glassy, and squared cut as I've always imagined houses in this neighborhood to be. It's the kind of house that would display well on an interior design magazine's cover—which, for all I know, it already has. And the pool is so big it could host an Olympic competition.

I'm stunned.

How much does a house like this cost?

It's intimidating.

"You must think I'm really dumb not to have known who Christian is," I tell Penelope as she parks.

"Aren't 'dumb' and 'rocket scientist' mutually exclusive?"

"Come on, you know what I mean."

"I think you're... different," she concedes. "And not in a bad way. The boss had a lot of the *same* pie and never quite bit into it. I've never seen him so taken by someone..."

"Yeah, the weirdo who had no idea who Christian Slade was."

"No." Penelope's turquoise eyes peer into mine. "The woman who liked him without knowing he's a famous actor."

I hope she's right. Anyway, I've procrastinated enough.

Time to go face the man.

"Should we go?" Penelope says, apparently reading my mind.

I nod and exit the car.

Penelope also climbs out, and tilts her head toward the house, saying, "This way, please, follow me."

I do, and we enter what could only be described as an atrium. The ceiling is double the height of a regular house, and the room stretches out into a gigantic open space that ends in a wall made entirely of glass with a magnificent view of the city below.

The décor is not my style, but I admit it has its charms. A bit cold and minimalistic, but with clean lines and a few warm touches that brighten the place up, like an abstract red painting that takes up almost the entire left wall, several vases filled with lush green plants, and golden and bronze metallic art sculptures resting on a cabinet near the couch.

I'm distracted from my scrutiny of the house by the light sound of footsteps coming down the stairs to the far right of the room. My heart leaps in my throat as the homeowner makes his appearance.

Christian hops down the last few steps and walks into the living room dressed more casually than I've ever seen him, in a white T-shirt and gray sweatpants.

He stops when he sees me, and we immediately lock gazes. Staring into his green-blue eyes is enough for the palpitations to start, and we aren't even breaking up. *What would happen to my heart if we were?*

The jitters worsen as Christian takes a few tentative steps toward me, then nods to Penelope. "Thank you, Penny, I can take it from here."

"All right, boss, I'll be in the office if you need me," she says, then turns to me and gives me a supportive arm squeeze. "Lana, it was a pleasure meeting you."

"Me, too," I say sincerely.

Penelope nods and disappears behind a door opposite the stairs.

"Hi," Christian says, closing the distance between us. "Thank you for coming."

He runs a hand through his thick hair, prompting a memory of me doing the same in a moment of passion last night, which only destabilizes me further.

"You must be really mad at me," he adds.

I swallow the emotions threatening to choke me. "More confused..." I say. "I had no clue. I feel so stupid..."

"Don't say that." He takes another step toward me so that we're only standing a foot apart now. "Never doubt yourself. You're the smartest woman I know."

"Academically, maybe, but I'm not street smart. Without Penelope's help, I wouldn't have been able to leave my house this morning."

"I'm so sorry for the ambush," he says earnestly. "It's all my fault. I never wanted you to find out like that."

Johnathan's words from when we broke up ring in my ears: *"That's not how we wanted you to find out."* No one ever wants me to discover things the way I do.

Count to ten, Lana.

I take a steadying breath, so as not to throw anger at Christian that's not entirely directed at him.

"So why not tell me?" I ask. "I can understand you're not used to having to tell people about"—I wave at the surrounding mansion—"all of this. But after the way we met, you must've known I value honesty above all else."

"I do, and I never wanted to lie to you." He gently grabs my hand, sending light tendrils of electricity coursing up my arm. "That's why I brought it up last night. I know you saying it was okay to wait didn't really make it okay for me not to tell you, but..." He takes a look at the room. "Can we please sit so I can explain?"

I nod and let him guide me to the angular white couch in the center of the room. We sit next to each other and I wait for him to talk.

"The last girlfriend I had, who I was sure was only interested in me for *me*, was in high school. I did my first movie when I was eighteen, and ever since then, I've been part of this glittering, smoke-and-mirrors world that is Hollywood. I've tried, but I've never been able to trust a woman 100 percent since I made it big."

"Why?"

"It's like being a rich guy and wondering if the woman you're with is only in it for the money. Except I'm both rich *and* famous, which is ten times worse."

I can't help but smirk a little at that. "Poor you," I say.

Christian grins. "Yeah, I guess I sounded like a major arse right there. And I'm not saying I'd rather not be rich or famous—acting has always been my dream, and I wouldn't give it up for the world. I'm only saying that, when it comes to relationships, I always have to wonder if a woman would still date me if I was a regular guy. With you, I never had to question your motives. And, as wrong as it was, I wanted to hold on to the sensation."

"But if we start playing the second-guessing game..." I frown and voice the doubt I've been keeping locked deep inside me since this morning. "I might begin to wonder if the only reason you're interested in me is *that* I didn't know who you were. For the novelty alone."

Christian reaches for my hands and presses his lips to my knuckles, sending my heart into a fast-beating frenzy. "That's not true," he says. "I like you for how beautiful and smart you are. Because you know how to be both serious and fun. For the secret smile that plays on your lips whenever you're thinking something the rest of the world doesn't know. For the blue of your eyes; I could get lost staring into them for hours. And, yes, also because you're as detached from Hollywood as a person could be."

Can I say he had me at *not true?*

"And you're kind and altruistic and share my values and causes," he continues.

"You a closeted green warrior as well?"

"No." He smirks. "But I'm the founder of Teachers Without Postcodes."

I frown, incredulous, as my heart skips a beat. "You are? But the charity is run by the Palmer Foundation."

"That's my mom's maiden name."

"Oh."

"I've been dying to tell you, to be someone you'd be proud of. And I promise I will never keep things from you in the future." When Christian delivers the final blow, I'm already a blushing, palpitating mess. He locks eyes with me, letting me see he's wearing his heart on his sleeve. "Can you forgive me?"

I'm about to say yes, to yell it so the whole city can hear, when we're interrupted.

"Have you decided on dinner, Mr. Slade?" someone asks.

I turn to look behind me, and...

"Chef Jeff!" I exclaim in surprise.

"Miss Lana. I mean, Lana... I... err..."

Christian's nostrils flare. "It's okay, Jeff, you can go. We can discuss dinner later..."

Looking crestfallen, Chef Jeff does half a bow with a nod at the end, then flees the room.

I look at Christian with a question mark stamped on my face.

"So." He grins devilishly. "There might be another small confession I have to make..."

18

LANA

"Stay," Christian asks.

We're in bed, my chin resting on his bare chest as he draws circles on my shoulder with a finger.

After our talk, it didn't take long for us to start making out on the couch, and one thing led to another...

Two hours later, I can certify that making love to Christian Slade the world-famous actor is no different from making love to Christian Slade the Hollywood wannabe. I felt no extra thrill, mostly because I think it'd be impossible to feel *more*. I swear I've reached the highest level of satisfaction a human being can achieve.

Although I have to say, having sex with other people present in the house—*personnel*—was weird. Christian's wealth still feels intimidating and makes me more uncomfortable than keen.

"I can't," I say, even if leaving my spot nestled in his arms is the last thing I want to do. "I have work tomorrow, and I have to feed the cats. Cengel and Boles are probably destroying the house already."

"Penny can go to your house, feed your darlings, and grab a

change of clothes for tomorrow. And she can drive you to campus again in the morning."

"Oh, I wouldn't want to inconvenience her. It's late."

"Don't worry, it's her job."

"To feed your girlfriends' cats?"

Oops, I said girlfriend. Too soon?

As usual, I blush.

But Christian immediately puts me at ease.

"Girlfriend, singular," he says, tapping my nose with one finger.

"Are you sure it's no trouble for her?"

"Penny is very well compensated for her efforts, and she knew this was a no-fixed-hours gig when she signed up. Trust me, she's happy to help."

"I'm not used to having people do things for me."

"So allow me to spoil you a little." Christian kisses my shoulder. "Being with me will have plenty of downsides; you witnessed some of those already. At least try to enjoy the perks." The cute frown that has become the bane of my existence makes an appearance. "Please, stay..." Christian whispers again.

How can I say no to that face?

Easy. I don't.

* * *

I end up staying at Christian's house the whole week. I still go to work—putting in all the hours, but afterward, it's right back to the mansion and into Christian's arms. By the time I walk back to my house, it's Friday night. I miss my cats, and they—well, they probably don't *miss* me, but they must have at least started fussing over where I've gotten myself off to. Penelope looked a bit frazzled the last time she returned from feeding them.

Christian offered to have Penelope give me a ride again, but I decided to do without the private chauffeur. To have an assistant by extension is weird. As is having a personal chef. And two maids, a gardener, a pool boy, a driver, and three rotating security guards. All those people at our beck and call. It's enough to make my head spin.

Also, I never imagined a house could require so many staff members to run. Being at Christian's feels more like staying at a hotel than visiting a boyfriend.

But at least there were no paparazzi.

Before getting home, I stop at the grocery store to grab something to eat tonight—what with not being able to order a custom dinner from the in-house chef—and loads of treats for Cengel and Boles. I expect the kitties to be epically mad at me for letting a stranger care for them for so many days without ever showing my face.

What I don't expect as I round the corner to my street, laden with grocery bags, is to find Johnathan seated on the front steps of the house.

I stop in my tracks, debating if I should duck around the corner and call Penelope to come to pick me up. A confrontation is the last thing I want. But I'm too slow; Johnathan raises his gaze and spots me.

No backing down, then. I sigh and, bracing myself, I reluctantly close the distance between us.

"What are you doing here?" I ask, skipping any form of polite greeting. The bastard gave up the right to even basic good manners when he cheated on me with my best friend.

"Is it true?" Johnathan brandishes a flashy magazine at me—it appears he, too, is in favor of skipping all social graces.

I drop the grocery bags on the landing to fish my keys out of my bag. "Is what true?"

He waves the cover of the magazine in my face. "You and that actor?"

My jaw drops as I stare at the patchwork of photos printed on the cover: a headshot of Christian, a picture of him leaving my house, one of me taken last Thursday morning about where I'm standing right now, and finally me and Penelope in Christian's car exiting his house two days ago. The title is printed in bright yellow all-caps characters across the page:

THE ROCKET SCIENTIST WHO STOLE CHRISTIAN SLADE'S HEART

Christian warned me stories about our relationship were bound to hit the news sooner or later. And I thought I was prepared, but it turns out that seeing my face on a magazine cover still feels surreal.

I snatch the magazine from my ex and flip to the feature page.

Hearts broke all over the world this week as news spread of six-times-in-a-row Sexiest Man Alive Christian Slade abandoning his bachelor life. It's official, ladies, Christian Slade is in a serious relationship with UCLA Ph.D. student Lana Voynich.

Voynich is a twenty-eight-year-old Westwood resident with no previous ties to Hollywood.

They lifted my headshot from the UCLA website and printed it side by side with another picture of Christian. I keep reading the article.

How the two love birds met remains a mystery, as neither Mr. Slade nor Miss Voynich were available for comment at the time this article was written.

Let's hope this is it for America's number-one heartthrob.
Too often in the past, we've seen his heart get broken...

The article continues with a recap of Christian's past relationships. On the right side of the page is another collage of broken-hearts photo frames of him with other women. *Many* other women. I count nine.

Are these all of his exes, or did they only choose to show the most significant ones?

How many women has he been with?

Again, I'm hit by how different we are. By how seasoned he is, and how inexperienced I am by comparison.

"So, is it true?" Johnathan's angry voice forces me to look up from the paper.

"What do you care?" I hiss.

"Wow, Lana, you were quick in moving on, huh?"

"What?" I bristle with indignation. "Should I remind you that you moved on while *we were still in a relationship*?"

A bright flash interrupts his reply.

"Trouble in paradise, Lana?" a guy holding a camera shouts from across the street. "Jealous ex-boyfriend?"

Another flash of the camera.

And as much as I don't want to, I'm forced to let Johnathan inside to avoid a public scene.

"Come in," I order, grabbing my groceries and elbowing my way through the door. "We can't do this outside."

"Wow, look at you," Johnathan says, following me inside and slamming the door shut behind him. "Already all VIP."

My ex takes a look at the almost entirely packed-up house and rears in shock. "Are you moving out?"

"Yeah, I can't afford the rent on my own."

"Are you moving in with *him*?"

"Not that it's any of your business, but no."

I drop the heavy bags on the kitchen floor and entrench myself behind the bar. "What do you want from me?" My voice rises higher than I'd like it to be. "You cheated on me with my best friend and made it perfectly clear you had no remorse about it. You were relieved I'd found out, Johnathan. *Relieved.*"

"So? What if I was wrong?"

"About what?"

"You... Us..."

"You're not making any sense."

"I know, but seeing you with that guy..." He grimaces.

"What?"

"I hate the idea of you dating other people. I don't want you to."

I used to love the way Johnathan said exactly what he was thinking without any filters. I thought it was brave. Now, it just comes off as selfish. And in this case, wildly deluded.

"Well, sorry, buddy," I snort. "You lost that privilege when you slept with Summer."

"I made a mistake, Lana. One mistake in ten years. *One.*"

"One too many, I'd say. Why are you here, Johnathan?" I ask again. "What do you want?"

"Seeing that article made me think... Maybe we were too quick in throwing away ten years after only a small bump in the road."

"Small bump?" I grab hold of the kitchen island to stop my hands from throwing things at his stupid face. "You call having a two-month affair with Summer a *small bump?* You really must be confused if you think there's even the slightest chance I'd get back together with you."

His expression darkens. "Of course, why would you, now that you have a celebrity boyfriend?"

"His fame has no meaning for me."

"What about your career then?"

"What about it?"

"Do you think anyone in academia will take you seriously after seeing your face plastered all over trash magazines?"

"Not everyone is as small-minded as you."

"Are you seriously ready to throw all your hard work and credibility out the window for a clown?" He's so angry literal spit comes out of his mouth. "And for what? How long do you think it'll last before he gets tired of you and goes back to dating someone in his league?"

"Wow, Johnathan, are you actually trying to win me back by insulting me? I can't believe I'm saying this, but I feel sorry for Summer; she deserves someone better than you." A horrible thought hits me. "Wait. Does she even know you're here?"

The flash of guilt that crosses his eyes is my answer.

"Oh my gosh, you're the worst," I say. "So now you're sneaking around behind her back, too? I'm sorry my best friend threw away a lifetime of friendship for you. And I'm sorry I wasted ten years of my life on you."

"*I* left *you*, remember that," he spits.

"Only after I caught you red-handed and asked you to leave. Best decision of my life." I fix him with the coldest glare I can muster. "So, I'll ask you again—what are you doing here?"

"Nothing, my bad," he says. But as he turns to leave, he mumbles something about a magazine. Doesn't take a rocket scientist—which I am—to figure out where his mind's at.

"Don't you dare go to the press with any of this," I warn.

"Or what?" Johnathan retorts. "What are you going to do?"

I have no answer for him. What *am* I going to do? What even *can* I do? It's not against the law to talk to the press, last time I checked. Even if it's my life he's talking about.

"That's what I thought." The bastard sneers and storms out of the house, slamming the door shut behind him.

I run to the window to check what he'll do next and, to my horror, see him handing a business card to the photographer still stationed outside.

What a jerk! Johnathan has never been perfect, but I never imagined him to be spiteful or vindictive.

I go back into the kitchen to feed the cats who, after witnessing the shouting match, are keeping a low profile. Cengel and Boles will save their complaints about my prolonged absence for another time. Once their bowls are full, I grab my phone and call Christian.

"Evening, beautiful. To what do I owe the pleasure?"

"We might have a problem," I say.

19

CHRISTIAN

As soon as I hear Lana's agitated tone, my heart drops.

I set aside my empty dinner plate and move outside to talk in private without Jeff overhearing.

"What happened?" I ask.

"My ex saw an article in a magazine about us and went nuts. He came to my house to yell at me—"

A surge of protectiveness swells in my chest. "Did he hurt you?"

"No, no. Nothing like that; he just wanted to rant. I'm not sure he even knew why he was here. He was confused; jealous, but confused. Anyway, we had a big fight, and there was a photographer outside the house. When Johnathan left, I saw him give the paparazzi his business card. You think the press would be interested in interviewing him? Can he cause trouble for you?"

The more I listen, the more I want to kick that bastard's ass to the curb.

"No, I'll make sure he doesn't go public," I say, and start to pace beside the pool.

"Are you sure?" Lana asks.

"Yes, I'll have my people sort it out. Don't worry, that bastard won't hurt you anymore, I promise. You want me to come over?"

"No, better not. I don't want the paparazzi to think you hang out here regularly; they're never going to leave me alone if you do."

That stings a little. "I can send Penny to pick you up, she's still here."

"I'd love to, but I'm exhausted. I could use a quiet night in…" I immediately worry that being in the limelight is already getting too much for Lana, when she adds, "Plus, we have a big night tomorrow." I hear the smile in her voice and relax. "I wouldn't want to make my public debut with bags under my eyes."

"Thank you for coming to the movie premiere with me. I know red carpets are not your thing."

"Christian, you're my thing," Lana says, "and that's all that matters."

And I swear I'm this close to telling her I love her, but I hold back. I can't do it over the phone.

"I'd better go now," Lana adds. "I need to convince Cengel and Boles I still love them, and that they still love me."

"All right. Penny will pick you up tomorrow at three. You're getting the VIP treatment. And don't worry about your ex; I'll take care of Johnathan."

"You sound like a Mob boss," she jokes. "Please don't murder him."

"I'll do my best not to. Can you give me his full name and address?"

"I don't know where he lives now. I haven't asked, and no one has told me. But I can text you his phone number if that's okay?"

"Perfect. I'll see you tomorrow, then."

"Can't wait."

"I'm going to miss you tonight."

"Me, too."

Her reply comes out in a low, sensual voice that makes me want to grab my car keys and race to her. But she asked for space and I must give it to her. We hang up, and I move into my home office, summoning Penny via text. She's using the gym before going home.

She pokes her head in twenty minutes later, droplets of water still glistening on her hair. "You called, boss?"

"Yeah, please sit." I gesture to the chair in front of me. "I need you to deal with something for me."

"When do you not..." She sighs, sitting. "What is it this time?"

"Lana's ex is proving to be... difficult. He threatened to go to the press. I'm not sure with what, but I want to avoid any blowbacks on Lana."

"So what's our strategy?"

"Pay him off," I say. "Alert the legal team and tell them to draft a non-disclosure agreement that covers his entire relationship with Lana: all ten years of it, plus recent events. I don't want him to be able to even speak her name in a public space."

"Okay. You want to review the agreement before the lawyers present it to him?"

"No." I cross my hands over the desk and lean forward on my elbows. "Penny, I want you to handle the ex in person. Make sure he signs."

"What if he doesn't?"

"Double the offer. I trust your negotiation skills."

"All right," Penny says, although her expression remains uncertain.

"You don't sound *all right*."

"It's just... Have you cleared this course of action with Lana? Is she okay with the payoff?"

"I told her I'd handle the situation, and that's what I'm doing. Why?"

"Yeah, but she might not be comfortable with your solution."

"Why not?"

"I don't know, boss, we're used to these kinds of deals. But maybe for other people, it isn't so normal to buy someone's silence." Penny bites the end of her plastic pen. "And I'm not positive Lana would want her ex to get paid for cheating on her."

"If he goes to the press, they'll pay him anyway. But the affair will become public knowledge. You think Lana would prefer that?"

"I think she'd prefer neither option."

"Well, unless you have another brilliant solution, please do as I say."

As Penny leaves, I dig my fingers into the chair's armrests. I hate how much the fame halo is already hurting Lana.

Hate it.

20

LANA

I spend the evening with my cats, catching up on my reading and letting the worries of the day slip away. I'm still in shock that Johnathan reacted so impulsively, and part of me can't help but wonder how low my ex is willing to sink.

I don't sleep well and the next morning, I wake up a little cranky, but at least I'm having coffee with Marjory at a quaint coffee shop doubling as a bookstore she suggested.

Marjory texts me that she's arrived early and is waiting for me at a table outside, so when I get to the shop, I stop at the counter and order a cappuccino and a croissant.

"Ten dollars, please," the barista says.

My eyes cross at the total, and I hate that I'm noticing these things now. That a simple coffee order makes me wonder if, when I meet with Marjory next year, I'll have to order the cheapest item on the menu because I'll be penniless. I take a sip of cappuccino, hoping it at least will be worth the $5.95 price tag. Thankfully, it's delicious.

I find my friend outside and plonk onto a chair next to her with a heavy, "Hey."

Marjory looks up from the romance novel she's reading and smiles. "Hey, Miss Famous, what's the latest with your love life? I can't keep up with all the news pieces coming out on you."

"You read gossip magazines?" I ask, surprised. I thought Marjory was all about books, a bit of a literary snob.

"Yeah, they're a guilty pleasure of mine. We get everything at the library and I just can't help myself. I swear you were on at least three covers this week alone."

I groan, but she's right. The tabloids are having a field day with my new relationship with Christian.

"Apparently you're not the only one enjoying gossip magazines."

She frowns interrogatively.

"Johnathan showed up at my house last night all riled up by an article; he threatened to go to the press himself. We had a huge argument with a paparazzi shark circling for blood outside my house."

Marjory nods. "I'm sorry. What did your ex want?"

I tell her the full story, and as I finish up, I'm relieved to have gotten it off my chest.

"Well, all I can say is that you have to be prepared for anything at this point." Marjory takes a sip of her coffee and nods sympathetically. "Maybe it won't be as bad as you think, but you need to stay vigilant and don't let Johnathan walk all over you. Don't let him get another piece of you and ruin your happiness."

I nod, relieved to have Marjory's support. "You're right. I just need to stay focused and keep my head up."

"That's the spirit," she says, smiling. "You can do anything you put your mind to. Take it one day at a time, and don't forget to enjoy the ride. You do have a pretty amazing one, after all."

I smile, thankful for her words of encouragement. It's good to know that no matter what I'm going through, I have Marjory in my corner. That even a new friendship can already feel this solid. I'll always have Winter as my best friend, but it's great to know I can still form deep and meaningful connections even without having known someone from childhood.

"Thanks, Marjory. That means a lot to me. Now, let's talk about something else. That weasel of my ex already stole enough of my time."

We spend the rest of breakfast discussing books and perusing together some of the gossip magazines Marjory mentioned. She can access them from the library website and gives me a rundown of all of Christian's famous exes and the alleged reasons why they broke up.

That's how I learn that the cheating girlfriend he referred to was in reality a famous co-star who cheated on him with another actor and that the scandal was a worldwide source of entertainment for the masses. My heart goes out to Christian. I mentally go back to our date on the beach, when he told me the story about his cheating ex. So when he said someone saw his girlfriend with another man, he must've been referring to this never-disappearing press carnage.

But mostly, Marjory and I have a good time poring over mindless gossip.

I end up leaving the coffee shop in a much better mood than when I arrived. For lunch, I eat a light salad, so as not to bloat up before I have to wear an evening gown. And at 3 p.m. on the dot, Penelope parks in front of my house.

Equally scared and excited about my first Hollywood outing, I get in the car and greet Christian's assistant with a big smile. "Hi."

"Hey." Penny beams back at me for a moment, then starts the car and sets us in motion.

"Is it really necessary to get ready all these hours in advance?" I ask, fastening my seat belt. "Just for a night at the movies?"

"Every spare minute. You'll see." She nods without taking her eyes off the road. "You're gonna love the special treatment."

I hope she's right because I'm the kind of person who cuts her hair once a year and finds even that tedious. How am I going to deal with hours of the *special treatment*?

And what is the special treatment, anyway?

I find out when we arrive at Christian's house. I barely have time to kiss him before I'm introduced to a stylist, a fretting-but-efficient-looking brunette with a tight chignon and a black pencil skirt suit.

"We're going to move to one of the guest bedrooms and choose the dress first," she informs me after introducing herself as Justine.

I turn to Christian, scared to be left alone with this clearly hyper woman. "You don't want to help pick a dress?" I ask hopefully.

"I can if you want," he says, "but I was kind of looking forward to it being a surprise."

And here comes the cute frown I can't say no to.

I nod. "Surprise it is, then."

Christian pulls me close and kisses me on the forehead. "I'll see you later."

With a sigh, I follow Justine to one of the *seven* guest rooms, where she hands over a white robe for me to change into.

Once I'm in the robe, I sit on the bed and wait as she rolls a rack of gowns to the center of the room.

"So," Justine says, clapping her hands. "Designers jumped at the chance to dress Christian Slade's new mystery woman, so you have a lot of options to choose from..."

I want to point out there's really nothing mysterious about me, but Justine doesn't seem the kind of person who likes to be contradicted, so I purse my lips.

She introduces each garment with a flourish, beginning the

description by name-dropping the designer. I try to arrange my features in an impressed expression, even if I don't recognize any of the big brands she seems so smitten with. I pay more attention to the description of the dresses for their own merits.

"Black is a classic," Justine says about the first dress. "Always flattering, looks good on anyone... although, admittedly, not the most daring choice."

She puts it back on the rack before I have a chance to formulate an opinion one way or the other.

I've got a feeling she's already picked a gown, and this presentation is pro forma. I'm tempted to tell her to stop right there and just tell me what I should wear, but she seems intent on saying her piece, so I keep quiet and nod as required.

"Blush is the second most obvious choice; this gown is amazing, of course, but the color is no statement. Now, this pale yellow one would put you on the fashion map for sure, but maybe not for a first appearance. And then we have this gold one, a real showstopper. And, finally, a pastel blue marvel that would do wonders to bring out your eye color."

If I'm following this right, she wants me to choose either the gold or the pale blue. Taking a chance, I say,

"Can I try the last two on?"

"Excellent choices," Justine says, who had already started to unzip the golden gown before I'd even made my request.

After a lot of fabric shuffling and zipper pulling, I change into the gold dress. It's gorgeous but too ostentatious for my liking. So I change into the blue one.

There's no contest.

I love the deep V neckline and the draped ruffles adorning the bodice, sleeves, and front slit skirt. And the color—periwinkle is the right name, Justine informs me—is adorable.

I stare at myself in the mirror wearing the pale blue gown

and know we have a winner. The gold dress was amazing, but this one seems tailor-made for me. The organza hugs my body in all the right places and flows to the ground as light as sea foam.

"Yeah." Justine appraises my reflection with a professional eye. "I had my money on this one, too. And we don't even need much tailoring. Teresa!"

A woman in her fifties hurries into the room carrying a sewing kit.

"Teresa will take your measurements and make a few adjustments," Justine says.

"Hi," I say to Teresa.

The seamstress nods at me in acknowledgment and asks me to stand on a small pedestal in front of the mirror. Everyone is so efficient and professional, it's kind of freaking me out.

"Have you already picked the shoes?" Teresa asks briskly. "I need you to wear them to fix the hemline."

"Oh, each dress came with its match," Justine says. "You're a size eight, right?"

Where she got this information is beyond me. I swear I've never discussed shoe sizes with Christian.

Justine pulls out a pair of stunning-but-impossible-to-walk-in silver sandals, and I stare in horror at the height of the stilettos.

"Mmm," I say. "Isn't there a pair with a lower heel?"

"Oh, darling, don't worry. You only have to walk the red carpet; you'll spend the rest of the night sitting. It'll be so brief, you won't even notice you have heels on."

I'm not sure I can manage even a short walk on those stilts, but, again, I keep my doubts to myself. I try the shoes on and do my best not to fall off the pedestal while Teresa shortens the hem of the dress and takes in the waist an inch.

Once the seamstress is done, Justine helps me take the gown

off, puts me back into the white robe, gives me slippers, and sends me off to the beauty team.

When I enter the next bedroom-turned-spa, I'm relieved to find Christian there, sprawled on a salon-like armchair.

"Hey, you," I say, smiling.

"Hey," he says, returning the smile. "Found a dress?"

"Yes. Thank you for all this." I gesture at the empty chair beside him, then sit down.

"Trust me, the pampering has only just begun."

We both get a foot massage, a facial, and a complete mani-pedi. Apparently, even male actors need to have perfectly mani-cured hands. By the end of the treatment, I'm so relaxed I feel more inclined to curl into bed with an herbal tea and my cats than going out. But, instead, I have to move on to hair and makeup. Who knew a night at the movies could involve so many prepara-tory steps.

The makeup artist doesn't consult me on what I want; instead, he checks a paper sheet Justine handed him and proceeds accord-ingly, as does the hairstylist. But I can't complain; the makeup is so subtle my face looks like I'm not wearing any, while the light retouches make all the difference. My cheekbones have never looked this sharp, and the blue mascara is making my eyes seem so big.

Same for the hair; it has never been so shiny and looks super lush in the loose, one-sided updo they've styled it into.

Once Justine declares me ready—a mere four hours after arriving at Christian's house—I stare in the mirror and almost don't recognize myself.

I thank Justine for all her work and, with a pounding heart, exit the room to go meet Christian in the living room.

He's standing at the foot of the stairs, and my heart positively stops as he turns around, his eyes widening as they meet mine.

In his sleek, dark tux, he's a sight to behold. And I don't care if he's famous, rich, or whatever else, because that blue-green gaze would always burn a hole through my soul no matter what.

His lips move in a silent "Wow" as he looks me over, and I hope the foundation they used is covering because my face flames tomato red.

I walk to him, and he pulls me close to give me a soft kiss on the mouth. "You look stunning," he breathes.

My heart is getting lost in another palpitating frenzy, so I try to make light of the situation. "It's what four hours of pampering will do for you."

Christian frowns. "Did you have fun?" he asks. "It wasn't too much?"

"I've never felt so spoiled in my entire life." That being said, I wouldn't want to sit through the whole shebang every weekend; hopefully, these red-carpet events aren't that frequent for Christian.

His face relaxes, and he says, "Should we?"

I nod, and, with a hand on my lower back, he ushers me toward the door.

There's a limousine waiting in the driveway. Apparently, celebrities don't go to movie premieres via Tesla. I bite my lip and don't complain about the carbon footprint, not wanting to spoil the atmosphere. But as I get in the car, I make a silent vow to enroll in the next beach clean-up volunteering event the city organizes to compensate.

Inside, the limousine is accessorized with a champagne bottle stored in a silver cooler and glasses. Christian pops the cork and pours us a glass.

"So, is this your first movie?" he asks, clinking his flute against mine.

"Not *ever*," I say. "But the first in many years, yes. So, what's the story about?"

"Any chance you read comics?"

"Nope." I laugh.

I spend the rest of the ride getting a crash course on super-heroes. Turns out they're a huge deal. Who knew? Christian claims his face is on cereal boxes. I need to go grocery shopping, stat.

The lesson ends when the limo stops in front of the Chinese Theatre, and we step out right onto the red carpet. Cameras flash at us from all directions, turning the dark night into a glittering day. Shouts of "Christian, this way please!" and, "Lana, look at me!" echo from all around us.

And, standing there in my beautiful dress, with a man who looks like a real-life prince, I feel like I'm living in one of the fairy tales I love so much to read.

I'm a nerdy frog turned princess.

I'm finally starting to get what all the fuss about Hollywood is. The glamour is already going to my head, making me excited and afraid at the same time. But I'm too busy smiling and trying to walk in these shoes without falling to dwell on what's happening.

Christian gives my arm a gentle tug and leans down to whisper in my ear, "Time to go. They've had enough."

I nod and follow him inside the theater. We stop in the entrance hall, and he asks again, "Are you sure it's not too much?"

"Positive. I'm having fun, I promise."

"You're a natural," he says, his voice full of pride. "And you're so beautiful."

Christian steals a kiss, and we walk into the main theater, where an usher guides us to our reserved seats.

Three hours later, we're still parked in our seats in the front row; the movie is *still* going. I'm having trouble keeping my back straight. The boning of the dress helps; it pokes me in the ribs whenever my shoulders sag. I try to covertly shift positions on the chair to give my butt cheeks a reprieve.

"It's almost over," Christian whispers.

His warm breath sears a path down my neck, making me want to slip out of this dress even more—and not just to get a break from the corset.

As promised, the movie soon ends. I can't say I enjoyed the plot, but seeing Christian in a tight spandex costume had its pluses. The audience must've loved it, though; they burst into applause as soon as the end credits start to roll. Christian stands up and gives them a cheeky wave, which provokes laughter and more applause.

To leave the theater, we're ushered out a side door and into a back alley where the limo is supposed to pick us up. The paparazzi must not know about this place, or possibly don't have access to it. Either way, I'm glad to avoid another encounter with dozens of flashing cameras.

As we wait, a thought suddenly pops into my head.

"Hey," I say. "I forgot to ask you. How did you handle things with Johnathan? Was he trouble?"

"Nothing to worry about. It's solved."

"Yeah, but how?"

"My people made him sign a non-disclosure agreement. He's legally bound not to speak about your relationship in public."

"And he signed it? Just like that?"

From the way Johnathan left my house yesterday, he didn't exactly seem open to being reasonable.

"He's agreed to," Christian says, his jaw tightening. "It's all that matters."

My heart sinks. "How?" I ask. "How did you convince him?"

Christian stares at me but keeps quiet.

So I prompt him. "I have a wild imagination." I try to phrase my mounting anxiety as lightly as possible. "If you don't tell me, I'll conjure up the worst scenarios..."

"I offered him money," Christian says at last.

"You paid him off? How much?"

"The same he'd get from a magazine for the story."

"Is it already done? Can you take the money back?"

"My lawyers are finalizing the papers over the weekend. He should sign them on Monday."

"Good." I kick a small pebble off the curb and almost lose my balance. "I want you to cancel the deal."

"Why? The money is nothing for me, I—"

"If you have so much cash to throw away, give it to charity," I interrupt.

"I already give a lot to charity," Christian snaps. "Why are you so mad?"

"Because..." I try to steady my breath and not kick anything else. "Excuse me if I don't want my cheating ex to receive a cash bonus as a reward for lying to me for months and for stealing my best friend."

Christian's hands cup my cheeks. "I've upset you. I'm sorry," he says. "But paying him is the only way. If he doesn't sign the agreement, your ex can go to a newspaper and sell the story. He'd get the same amount of money anyway, except he'd also drag your name through the mud in the process."

"Drag me through the mud, how? I've done nothing wrong; *he's* the shady one. If he wants to confess his affair in front of the entire world, he can be my guest."

Christian sighs. "That's not how it works. You're assuming he'll go to the papers and tell the truth. Most people don't. Especially not the ones holding a grudge. He could tell a magazine all kinds of lies."

"I don't care. I want you to cancel the deal."

"Are you sure? If he goes to the press... Once something has been printed, there's no way of burying the story. And even if you go public with a different version, there's no guarantee people will believe you over him. The blowback could get ugly with social media and all that stuff... It might even affect your job..."

The thought of Johnathan spinning lies on the news makes my blood boil, but I refuse on principle to let my boyfriend pay him off. He won't get a cent from Christian, end of the story.

"I'm sure," I say, gathering my hem up as the limo pulls up next to us. "Whatever lies Johnathan feeds the papers, I can deal with it."

"As you wish," Christian says, leaning down to kiss me on the forehead. "I'll call the legal team tomorrow and make sure they cancel everything. Now, let's go home."

I lean into his reassuring warmth for a short moment before we get into the limousine.

* * *

"Join me for a drink?" Christian asks as we step out of the limo at his house. "The view is amazing at night."

"Sure," I say.

"Wait here." He guides me toward the plush chairs lining the pool. "I'll be back in a sec."

I gladly take the chance to sit and give my feet a rest. True, I've spent most of the evening seated, but these shoes are real killers. I massage my ankles and take in once more the massive house, glittering pool, and landscaped garden... Could this really be my life? Would I want it to be?

I don't know. The argument about Johnathan added a sour note to an otherwise perfect night, reinforcing my theory that I'd like Christian better if he weren't a famous actor.

The stress from the paparazzi trailing our every move. The thought that, for him, having a legal team buy the silence of my ex is par for the course. It's all just so outside my quiet life as an academic. Could I ever get used to this lifestyle? No, I'm pretty sure I'll never find this life normal. But for him, I can try to cope.

"Want a glass of champagne?"

I look up to find Christian towering over me, a dark green bottle and two glasses in his hands.

I smile. "What could ever go wrong with that?"

Christian grins back. "Oh, several things."

"Like what?"

"I could pull a *Sabrina* on you."

"I have no idea what you're talking about."

"*Sabrina*—the movie, with Audrey Hepburn?"

"Sorry, I don't—"

"—watch TV," he finishes for me. "But *Sabrina* is a classic; you have to see it. At least once."

"All right. So, what happens that's so terrible to this Sabrina that involves champagne?"

"To her, nothing. But the poor fella forgets he's put glasses in his pockets, and sits down on the tennis court, and..."

"Ouch!"

"But no tennis courts here, so we're safe. Come see the view?"

I push off the chair and, as we come face to face, I have to steady my legs—and not just because of the heels. Even in the semi-dark, Christian's eyes are so intense...

Too soon to feel so much, Lana. Definitely too soon.

But when I'm around him, my heart swells in my chest until my rib cage seems too small, while a dark snake of fear coils in my stomach and hisses a silent question over and over again:

How much are you going to hurt me?

21

CHRISTIAN

I lead Lana to the open terrace and, using the concrete railing as a makeshift table, I pour the champagne and hand her a glass.

Somehow, I sense the atmosphere has shifted; it's suddenly laden with meaning. *Serious.* This thing between us is progressing at a speed I wasn't prepared for. A pace I can't slow down.

And why should I?

As her intelligent sapphire eyes fix on me, I find I have to keep my tongue in check so as not to make a complete fool of myself. Instead of offering her a drink, I almost came out and told Lana I'm in love with her.

Way too soon, mate, to even be thinking along those lines.

Right. But with Lana, it's impossible not to burn the stops. I'd forgotten how exciting the chase could be. For the first time in forever, I don't have the upper hand in a relationship. My career, fame, and money mean nothing to her. It's refreshing, exciting, unsettling, and, yes, a bit scary, to be honest.

"What are we toasting to?" Lana asks.

"To a perfect evening with a perfect woman," I say. "Thank you for coming with me tonight."

"I'm not perfect." I watch her cheeks redden in the cutest possible way. "And, thank *you*. This whole day has been incredible. Surreal, but amazing."

"Cheers."

We clink glasses and I pull her closer, hugging her from behind as we stare at the city lights sparkling below us.

I press my lips to the side of her neck. "You've gone awfully quiet," I say.

I almost expect her to tell me something grave, but she surprises me by saying, "I was trying to remember what the view from your bedroom is."

I hear the smile in her reply, and imagine her mouth curled into that secret grin of hers while her actual words set me on fire. "I also seem to be suffering from a case of amnesia," I say. "'Cause I can't remember, either. Should we go check it out?"

She turns in my arms, her smile fading only when she kisses me and whispers, "Sure."

* * *

The next morning we wake up late and linger in bed—*not sleeping* —longer still. We eventually venture downstairs for a lush brunch, courtesy of Jeff, when Penny arrives carrying her tablet with her.

"Morning, boss, Lana." My assistant sits at the kitchen island with us and helps herself to a slice of French toast.

"Don't you ever get a day off?" Lana asks. Slanting her eyes at me in a teasing manner, she adds, "You're a slave driver."

"Am not," I defend. "She gets plenty of days off."

"Do I?" Penny asks jokingly.

"Yeah, you get Christmas every single year, and I think I gave you Thanksgiving off that one time."

Lana shakes her head, amused, and keeps enjoying her cinnamon roll.

Penny sticks out her tongue at me. "You deserve all the mean tweets you get. Want to see the Jimmy Kimmel replay? It aired on Friday."

"Sure," I say.

Grabbing the remote, she screen-mirrors her tablet to the kitchen TV and shows us the clip.

My face appears on the screen with a brick wall in the background as I read the mean tweet: *"Christian Slade has the face of a dude who'd request She Bangs at a wedding and then try to salsa dance with a bridesmaid when the music isn't salsa and he can't even dance."* In the video, I scoff/smile, and say, *"You're right, mate. I can't salsa dance."*

We all laugh, and Lana asks, "Do people really waste time writing stuff like that?"

"You've no idea," I say.

"At least they're original," Penny adds.

"And how's the coverage from last night?" I ask her.

"Mostly positive." She scrolls through various news pieces about the movie premiere. There are pictures of me and Lana on the red carpet—she's even more stunning than I remembered—and the headlines are a variation of the same Christian Slade's new movie/new relationship.

Penny stops the slideshow and I see her looking at me, uncertain.

"What?" I ask.

"There's one final piece that isn't exactly flattering."

"Show us," I prompt.

She swipes left on the tablet, and a picture of me and Lana in the back alley waiting for the limousine appears. Lana looks angry and ready to cry and I look, well, like I swallowed ten lemons. The headline reads: "Is the fairy tale over already?"

"Wow," Lana says next to me. "How did they get that? Wasn't that alley off-limits for the press?"

"It was," I confirm. "But the paps would go to any lengths to steal a money-making shot. From the angle of the picture, it looks like the photo was taken from above; they must've been perched on a nearby roof."

"Is a shot like that really worth a lot?" Lana asks.

"Ten K at least," Penny says.

"What a waste of money. Do people really care?"

"Gossip sells." I shrug. "And bad news sells more than happily ever afters. This is what I was trying to tell you yesterday; the press doesn't care about the truth. They take a moment like that and turn it into whatever crap they feel like spinning that day."

"You want me to respond, boss?" Penelope asks.

"No, I don't think so." I turn to Lana for confirmation, and she shakes her head in agreement with me. "Are you sure you still want to cancel the Johnathan deal?" I ask.

"One hundred percent," Lana confirms immediately. "He's not getting a cent out of you, and if someone else wants to pay him to badmouth me, at least it won't be your money. He can tell all the lies he wants; I know the truth, and I don't care."

I take a sip of coffee and try to phrase my doubts tactfully. "But your family, your friends, your colleagues, your students... They won't know who to believe. Are you sure you want your private life put on display like that? I can make it all disappear. Why not let me?"

Her features set in the most adorable, serious pout. "Johnathan isn't getting any money from you, full stop."

"All right." I sigh. "Penny, can you have the legal team cancel the deal, please?"

Penny's lips curl up into the slightest I-respectfully-told-you-so grin, and she nods once. "Consider it done, boss." Then she turns to Lana. "You think your ex would really go public with the story?"

"I'd say no." Lana shrugs, taking a sip of coffee. "But a month ago I would've also told you he'd never cheat on me with my best friend, so…"

22

LANA

Johnathan's interview goes public two weeks later, and on my birthday, no less.

Worst timing ever, as I'm home celebrating with my family when the scandal breaks. Usually, our middle-aged neighbors in the Pasadena suburb where my parents live don't bother to read trashy magazines. So my relationship with a Hollywood A-lister had escaped their notice so far. But with two families on the block involved, Johnathan's piece cracks the suburban indifference wall, leaving me to deal with the fallout completely alone.

Of the two people mentioned in the article, I'm the only gossiped-about daughter present. Summer, as an excuse not to attend my birthday party—a first in over twenty years of friend-ship—claimed to be on a business trip. The excuse was given not to me—I still haven't heard a peep from her—but to her family.

Not that they believed her.

When Winter and I arrived home Friday night—we carpooled here together from our new shared apartment; we're now officially roommates—Mrs. Knowles, the twins' mom, interrogated us about Summer's absence. But we both maintained a code of silence, not giving away anything of what had transpired in LA. Little did we know the topic was about to become public knowledge.

One housewife recognizing my picture in a magazine Saturday morning was enough for the juicy story to spread like wildfire until the whole neighborhood became versed in my personal life.

And it's a disaster.

The Knowles still live next door to my family. And while Summer's mother gave her daughter a tongue-lashing in private— Winter overheard them and told me—she still felt compelled to defend Summer in public. Which resulted in a major argument between her and my mother. The moms' showdown took place at the annual charity bake sale on Sunday in front of the entire community.

Afterward, Mom kindly thanked me for ruining her favorite event of the year.

Now the neighborhood is split into factions. While no one condones cheating, it's clear some of my parents' neighbors believed Johnathan's version of our breakup. In the article, he depicted me as a workaholic ice queen, while he described himself as a poor, starved-for-affection man who'd made a mistake. The wording made it sound as if *he* was the victim.

Mom, besides blaming me for the bake sale fiasco, claims all the attention to be impossibly harassing. Personally, I think she loves being in the spotlight, especially since she's fighting from the moral high ground.

But, honestly, they are all a bunch of old gossips who have never enjoyed themselves more. They revel in the scandal, and everyone likes to play devil's advocate and give their two cents—*to me*, unfortunately.

The mayhem of these two days makes me reconsider my decision of stopping Christian from blocking the story. Now I get what he was trying to warn me about. But all considered, I stand by my choice; the idea of Johnathan getting money from my boyfriend remains more disturbing than the scandal.

Still, when I board the bus to get back to LA on Sunday evening—Winter had to go back earlier to catch a flight to Bangkok—I've never been happier to leave my hometown.

* * *

When I get off the bus in LA I'm surprised to find Bill, Christian's driver, waiting at the station for me. Christian had offered to have his chauffeur drive me to and from Pasadena, but I'd refused. Naïve me thought arriving home escorted by my boyfriend's driver would raise too many questions.

Ah!

Plus Winter drives a hybrid, so it was okay to carpool on the way there.

"Hi, Bill," I say, going to him.

"Good evening, Miss Voynich."

"How many times do I have to tell you? Please call me Lana." I stop in front of him. "What's the message?"

He smirks. "Mr. Slade has asked me to inform you the cats are fed and cuddled, while he has remained cuddle-less for three days."

I cross my arms, suppressing a grin. "Has he now?"

"And even though you have plans to celebrate your birthday tomorrow evening, Mr. Slade has taken the liberty to commission Chef Jeff's famous red velvet cake, if you wanted to blow out a candle tonight."

Homemade—or should I say, chef-made—red velvet cake? The man plays dirty.

I hand Bill my suitcase, knowing there'd be no point in trying to carry it myself, and follow him to the Tesla.

23

CHRISTIAN

"I missed you." I go to Lana the moment she walks into my house and pull her in for a kiss.

She's slightly rigid at first but then relaxes into my arms, the tension in her shoulders leaving her.

"How are you?" I ask.

"Better now that I'm with you."

We kiss again, ending in a long hug.

"I'm sorry about the article," I whisper in her ear.

Lana pulls back, cupping my cheek. "Hey, you had nothing to do with it. If anything, I'm responsible for not realizing I spent ten years of my life next to a man who willingly participated in an interview meant to humiliate me."

"Oh, baby, it's not your fault."

"It isn't," she concurs. "Let's agree it's all Johnathan's fault and not give him the satisfaction of ruining our night."

"Are you hungry? Did you have dinner already?"

"I ate at my parents'." Lana's mouth curls into that secret smile of hers. "I came here only for dessert."

I smirk. "In that case, let's go outside."

I guide her to the small table I'd laid outside with her birthday cake and a bottle of champagne.

"Christian, this is gorgeous," she says, taking in the perimeter of the pool lined with candles, and the fairy lights strung over the trees.

"I figured we might celebrate in style," I explain.

I help her sit, then uncork the champagne and pour us each a glass.

"Happy birthday, baby." I hand her a flute.

She gives me a slow smile and motions with her glass. "To us."

"To us."

After taking a sip of champagne, we dig into the cake, which is as good as Jeff had promised me.

"Mmm, it's delicious," Lana says, licking her lips.

"Told you." I laugh, taking a bite.

We sit in comfortable silence for a few minutes, until Lana looks up at me. "Thank you, I really needed a pick-me-up after the bumpy weekend."

Again, my heart cracks that she has to endure the repercussions of me being a celebrity, but I try to keep the conversation light.

"Any time you need a pick-me-up, I'm here for you."

"I know." She smiles, her gaze on me.

This is what I want—to be here for her, to make her feel safe and loved, to give her the best life I can.

"And now, I believe I have something else for you," I say, reaching for the gift-wrapped present I hid under the table.

"Christian..."

"Open it," I urge, and hand the large box to her.

Lana takes it, her eyes already wide with excitement.

I hold my breath as she rips the paper open. Will she like it?

* * *

"Did Lana like her present?" Penny asks me first thing as she barrels into my office on Monday morning.

"Mmm, yeah... She, mmm, thought it was cool, yeah."

To be honest, Lana's reaction was... not what I had expected.

"She had no idea, right?" My assistant nails the issue.

"No, I don't think she had a clue. I don't even know if she likes the bag."

"Ah, boss, you should've known better." Penny scoffs. "You wanted someone who didn't like you for your money... Sorry, but that means you have to put in the work now when you buy presents. The price tag doesn't matter anymore; you need to find something meaningful."

"Like what?"

"Boss, I can't tell you what to get. You're the one in a relationship with Lana; think of something she'd like. But it has to be relevant. As Britney said, *you gotta work, bitch.*"

What do they say? Careful what you wish for...

"How about the other issue?" Penny asks. "Was Lana upset?"

"She said the weekend at home was *bumpy,* but she brushed off most of my questions about the ex news piece."

"And what's your take?"

"The article hit her harder than she expected, but she still wouldn't have wanted me to pay a cent to her ex. And I have to respect her decision."

Penny sighs. "I hope the gossip meat grinder doesn't get too much for her..."

Yeah, I add silently inside my head, *me, too.*

24

LANA

"Does anyone have questions?" I ask after finishing my explanation of fluid viscosity.

A bunch of hands shoot in the air.

"Jordan," I say, addressing the punk-looking kid in the first row. "You go first."

"Are you really Christian Slade's girlfriend?"

The question takes me by surprise and, damn it, now I'm blushing in front of my students. "That's none of your business," I say. "And it's outside the scope of this lecture. Monroe, what's your question?"

"What's it like to date a celebrity?" the skinny young woman in the second row asks.

"Is he as hot in person as he looks on TV?" someone else shouts from the back of the classroom.

"Does Christian have any secret tattoos?"

My nostrils flare, and I cut the discussion before it can run even more out of control. "Does anyone have a question *not* related to Christian Slade?"

About half the hands in the classroom lower.

"Adams," I fire next.

"Did your boyfriend really cheat on you with your best friend?"

This disturbing new trend of asking personal questions needs to be shut down at once.

"Guys," I address the class at large. "My life outside this class is not up for discussion. So please stop asking inappropriate questions." I pause to let the message sink in, then ask, "Does anyone have a question about viscosity?"

There's a general murmur of discontent and all hands flop down disappointed, except for one.

"Yes, Chang?"

"Is dynamic viscosity dependent on temperature as well?"

"Great question," I say, relieved we're back on solid—or, rather, *fluid*—ground. "And the answer is yes. Dynamic viscosity is a function of kinematic viscosity and can be calculated as the product of kinematic viscosity and density. So both these quantities are influenced by the temperature. This brings us to the second part of the lecture..."

I write a list of discussion points on the board and address them as I go. "Is it better to have a low or high temperature for fluid motion? What are the advantages of both, and what happens in extreme heat conditions like, say, in a turbine? Or at the opposite end of the spectrum when the temperature drops below zero? Like it happens in certain conditions in space, and the temperature plummets, reaching values lower than minus one hundred degrees Celsius." Turning to the class, I ask, "Can anyone guess the answers?"

Thankfully, the debate keeps my students' brains stimulated enough to avoid any further attempts at discussing my love life. And I don't even have to resort to more serious threats—like extra homework—to keep them disciplined.

* * *

Once the class is over, I exit the Engineering Department and head toward my favorite café to have lunch. I'm walking across campus when a random student falls into step next to me.

"You're that professor, right?" he asks. "The one in the paper."

"You read my article in *Engineering Science and Technology*?" I ask. "Are you a student of mine?"

The guy seems puzzled for a second as if I'm speaking Arabic to him. "No, I meant you're the one dating Christian Slade. You were on the cover of *OK!* this week. Hey, can I take a selfie with you?" And before I can say no, he's already taken out his phone, placed his face inappropriately close to mine, and he's snapping away. "Cool," he concludes after taking a few shots. "See you later."

And as quickly as he arrived, the boy is gone.

How people can care so much about a complete stranger's personal life is really beyond me. I mean, what's the point of knowing which celebrity is dating who, if you don't know any of them?

"People are bored with their lives," I remember Penelope telling me. *"Your relationship gives them a thrill. Christian dating a non-celebrity is on the same scale as a prince marrying a commoner; it makes every woman on the globe dream about becoming a princess. And when the story turns from a fairy tale into an ugly breakup, it comforts people that even the rich and famous experience heartbreak. It makes them feel less alone."*

I'm still not convinced, but, for my relationship's sake, I need to learn how to grapple with the unwanted attention.

I reach the café, order a veggie sandwich, and fish my phone out of my bag to pay. My *new* bag. Christian's present for my birthday.

I stroke the red leather with my fingertips, and sigh. It's a nice bag, really. Undoubtedly some expensive designer brand. I shouldn't complain. But even so, it felt a little impersonal, as presents go. I mean, even Johnathan the Cheater was slightly better at choosing gifts. Last year, he got me a cute pink T-shirt with "I love you" written in binary code.

That being said, Johnathan has known me for ten years, whereas Christian and I have been dating for barely a month and a half. I should give his gift-making skills time to grow. And to be fair, my ex and I came out of the same nerdy pool; I can't expect everyone to get excited about binary code.

"Anything to drink?" the woman behind the counter asks me.

"No, thank you," I say. "I have my own water."

Single-use plastic bottles are as bad for the planet as gas-powered cars.

The woman pushes a few buttons on the cash register and smiles. "Go ahead."

I scan the code on my phone and sink it back into my bag.

"Veggie sandwich for Lana," a guy shouts from behind the counter.

I grab my sandwich and move outside to eat in the sun.

I haven't been seated for two minutes when my resolution to learn how to deal with unwanted attention is already put to the test. Hard as I try, I can't ignore the cluster of students sitting at the table next to mine who are clearly gossiping about me. It's obvious from the way they whisper to each other, heads bent close together, and keep throwing furtive stares my way.

No, they're not bothering me. I'm letting it go. I'll sit here and eat my meal without paying attention to—

"Excuse me?"

Sticking to my resolutions becomes impossible when one of the young women—a tall, lean blonde—approaches me directly.

"Yes?" I say, staring up at her.

"Sorry to bother you," she says. "But my friends and I..." I'm expecting the are-you-that-professor-dating-the-famous-actor question, when she surprises me by saying, "We couldn't stop looking at your bag. Is that the real thing?"

I throw a glance at the red bag sitting on the chair next to mine and blink. "What do you mean, the *real thing*?"

"Is the bag original? Or is it a knockoff?" she asks, and I only have a moment to think, *What a rude question*, before she adds, "If it's a fake, it's an impressive one."

Should I thank her for saying my allegedly fake bag looks like a really nice copy?

Christian doesn't seem like the kind of guy who buys counterfeit presents, so I say, "I think it's real. But I don't know, really, it was a present."

"Oh my gosh." Her excitement turns up a notch. "Your boyfriend must be loaded."

After a moment of shock at the even more blatant rudeness of the comment, my first instinct is to counter that, no, my boyfriend isn't loaded. But then I remember that Christian is, indeed, rich.

The young woman must read the answer on my face, and also the confusion, because she says, "Wait, you know that bag is an Angelika Black 901 limited edition, right?"

"Well, I know now," I say, failing to keep the irritation from my voice. "What's so special about it?"

"What's so special...?" She scoffs, incredulous. "Only that it's one of the most exclusive fashion pieces on the planet. You can't buy that bag in a shop; the waiting list is, like, five years long, at least." Then I see a flash of shrewdness pass through her eyes. "I'll tell you what; I'll give you five thousand dollars for it right now."

Five thousand dollars, for a bag?

I hate that my first instinct is to convert the amount to how many months of rent it'd cover. Next, I think she must be crazy to offer me that much. But then I give her a better look, taking in her expensive-looking clothes and shoes. She must know what she's talking about. But there's something about the sly light in her eyes that tells me she's conning me somehow.

"Sorry," I say. "The bag's not for sale. As I said, it was a present."

Her evil little grin dies on her lips and she grimaces, saying, "Your loss, lady." Then she turns on her heel and rejoins her group of friends.

And no matter how lovely the day is, I don't want to stick around and overhear a bunch of twenty-year-olds mock the lady who didn't know she had a five-thousand-dollar bag. So I go back to the lab, angle my screen so that the other Ph.D. students won't see what pages I'm looking at, and, once again, I'm in front of the old sage, knower-of-it-all, Google, to be enlightened.

I type Angelika Black 901 bag in the search box.

About 41,000,000 results (0.41 seconds)

My gaze drifts at once to the eBay ads windows. There are three bags on sale like mine going respectively for $22,000, $23,550, and $21,000. Apparently, that canny blonde was trying to short-change me by over $15,000. No wonder she was so angry when it didn't work.

But the unsuccessful con artist wannabe is the least of my problems right now. If I thought a bag wasn't much of a present for my birthday, Christian must really have no idea who I am to buy me something so expensive.

How could he think I'd like it? I almost find it offensive for a bag to cost as much as—or even more than—a car. The amount could repay two years of student loans, or pay for a year of rent, and it's a little over half my yearly salary.

And then I get irrationally mad. I don't know why. Maybe because I'm scared. The bag seems like a glaring red leather flag signaling Christian and I don't belong together. That our worlds sit a universe apart, that I'll never fit into his starry kingdom made of mansions, red carpet events, and twenty-thousand-dollar bags.

The halo of doom and gloom stays with me throughout the afternoon. No one shows up for office hours, leaving me trapped alone inside my head and too distracted to complete any real experimental work.

The bag also makes me curious about the women he dated before. Were they all designer clothes types? The lack of interruptions enables me to dig into Christian's past in depth. After all, his exes are just a click away, forever recorded on the internet for everyone to read about. So I do.

I confirm what I'd already glimpsed with Marjory. All his past love stories seem to follow the same hyperbole: the secrets and rumors phase, followed by the official, openly dating and happy phase, and then a press release about the relationship being over, accompanied by endless speculation on why it ended.

They all follow this pattern, except for his relationship with that actress who cheated on him.

She's one of several actresses he's dated, but of all his exes, she's definitely the most intimidating. Strikingly beautiful, but with a wholesome, girl-next-door look that makes her even more attractive. Big smile, dark blonde hair with highlights, light blue eyes.

This relationship gets by far the most attention—not because it's so different from the others, but for the way it ended when she was caught cheating on him by the paparazzi. People really have a taste for drama.

My head spins with all the new info, and to save myself from permanent brain damage, I shut my laptop and concentrate on the only work I can do mechanically: grading homework.

The temporary distraction is not enough to erase the side effects of my rampant soul-searching and Google searching. So, when I walk out of the lab later that evening, I'm still in an awful mood.

Christian and I are supposed to have dinner for my birthday tonight, but I'm not in the state of mind to celebrate.

Penelope is waiting for me, parked in the usual spot. I get in the car, mumble a hello, and keep staring out the window, morose.

She must notice my attitude because, halfway to Christian's house, she asks, "Are you okay?"

"Did you know this is a twenty-thousand-dollar bag?" I ask, pointing at the offending piece of fashion.

"Ah, yes, you found out." She keeps her eyes on the road, her expression unreadable. "You don't like the concept, I take it?"

"It's so..."

"Over the top?" Penelope suggests.

"To say the least."

"In his defense, when you earn as much as Christian does, for as long as he has, it's difficult to remain in touch with the reality of most people. To him, that bag is spare change."

"Well, to me, it's a year's rent," I say, indignant.

"You should probably discuss this with him."

"Oh, I will."

We stop at a red light and Penelope types something on her phone. I don't feel comfortable enough with Christian's assistant to lecture her on texting and driving, which only makes me angrier. I hate when people think their messages can't wait ten minutes to be sent. *What does she have to text that's so important, anyway?*

25

CHRISTIAN

I'm at home, nervously waiting for Lana and Penny to get here after the present fiasco of last night when my phone pings with a short text from my assistant. A warning.

FROM PENNY

L knows about bag

Pissed

Shit.

Lana found out how much the bag is worth. I wonder how. I also hope that my second present will make up for dropping the ball on the first.

The ladies arrive ten minutes later, and I wouldn't have needed Penny's text to see that something's wrong with Lana.

"Hi," she greets me, along with a quick kiss on the cheek.

"You're mad," I say.

I like that I can be direct with her. That she actually prefers it that way. No need to circle around things.

"More like overwhelmed," Lana says, equally direct.

"What happened?"

She launches into a ramble about inopportune questions during a lecture, boys taking sneak selfies, and a student offering her five thousand dollars for the bag. "I mean," Lana concludes, "you know the neighborhoods I go to for my volunteering; they could've shot me dead for a bag worth this much."

Oh, I hadn't thought of that.

"Sorry," I say. "That was stupid of me."

"I get that you wanted to give me a special birthday present, I really do. But something so flashy... It's not me. I'm here struggling to find funds to finish my Ph.D., I could be jobless next year, I could have to take on more student loans, I don't even know if I'll be able to afford a frigging five-dollar cappuccino, and you gift me a twenty-thousand-dollar bag?"

I'm taken aback by the impetuous of her rant. When she told me she'd lost her funding, I hadn't understood her entire career was at risk.

"I'm sorry, I didn't know the situation at work was so serious. You never talk about it; I thought the grant thing was resolved."

She grabs her chin and paces as if wanting to calm herself before she speaks next. "I never talk about it because I know you'd just offer to cover my grant, and I don't want that."

I know it shouldn't, but her statement hurts a little. "Why not?"

"Because it'd ruin the balance in our relationship. Because then I'd owe you, and I don't think that would be good for us."

I agree. I go to her and hug her. "I'm sorry I didn't see how worried you were, and I'm sorry you didn't feel you could open up to me about it." I gently grab her shoulders so she has to look up at me. "And I'm even more sorry I'm an idiot who flaunted a twenty-thousand-dollar bag in your face."

Her features soften. "I'm sorry, too. I can't *not* tell you things and expect you to know them anyway."

"Is there any way I can help you with the grant?"

"No, don't worry, I'm still working on finding a sponsor." She gives me a little smile, *finally.* "But if you have a billionaire friend with a kink for outer space, please send them my way. I won't take your money, but I'll gladly take theirs."

She kisses me, and I pull her closer.

When we pull apart, the air between us is still a little rough, so I tilt my head and ask, "Would it help if I said I'd already realized my mistake with the bag and bought you a second, incredibly cheesy and soppy present...?" And before she can say anything, I add, "Price tag under a hundred bucks, I swear."

Lana tries to keep serious, but a smile pulls at the corners of her mouth. "It would."

I nuzzle her neck. "And what should we do with the bag?"

Lana looks up at me, big sapphire eyes I can't say no to peering into mine. "Can we auction it off, give the proceeds to one of your charter schools, or to an environmental group?"

"I can make donations to all those causes and you can keep the bag; no need for an auction."

"I'm not comfortable walking around with twenty thousand dollars on my shoulder."

"And selling the bag would make you happy?"

"Immensely so."

"Consider it done."

I hug her tight, thinking I really don't deserve this woman. When I try to let her go, Lana pulls me back into a kiss, peace made.

"So," she says with a smile. "What is this other incredibly cheesy, soppy, and cheap present you were talking about?"

"Ah, it needs a special setting to be delivered properly. You still want to have dinner with me?"

"Of course I do."

"Then I'll get the Tesla's key card from Penny and we can go."

"I have to say." Lana pats me on the shoulder. "For someone who buys twenty-thousand-dollar bags, you have a pretty sensible taste in cars."

My smile falters.

To tell her, or not to tell her?

I decide honesty is the best policy here. "About that." I run a hand through my hair. "The Tesla might be *one* of the cars I own."

Lana frowns. "How many do you have?"

Gosh, I really hope she won't hate me. "It's double digits."

"Ten?" Lana asks, astonished.

"Uh... try twice that?"

Her mouth forms the cutest O of surprise. Then she shakes her head in a you're-impossible way. "What's your favorite?" she asks.

"Definitely the Ferrari."

"You own a Ferrari?" Her eyes shine.

"Err, if you want, we could change the ride? Leave the Tesla just for tonight?"

"Aww." Lana bites her lower lip. "You're corrupting all my principles here. It's hard to resist the seduction."

And like the devil I am, I whisper in her ear, "It'd be only this once. It's your birthday; you deserve to have fun." She still seems undecided, so I add, "I promise I'll do something environmentally friendly in return to balance out your transgression."

"Like what?"

"I could challenge all my followers not to use their cars for a day."

"And they'd do it?"

"Not all, but some, for sure."

"How many followers do you have?"

"One hundred and thirty-five million..." I don't even try for faux modesty. "Give or take."

Her jaw drops. "That's a whole nation and not even a small one." I can almost hear the cogs in her brain turning, making calculations. "Even if only 1 percent accepted your challenge... that'd still be over a million people not driving for an entire day." And finally, with a big smile, Lana says, "Now I have to try the Ferrari, for the good of the environment."

I grin back. "You basically have no choice. I'll ask Bill to bring it out."

Five minutes later, we're standing in the driveway next to the Ferrari. Lana approaches it almost reverentially.

She wrings her hands nervously. "Would you mind if... I mean, could I have a look inside?"

The question puzzles me. *Aren't we getting in, like, right now?* But I nod and unlock the car for her.

Lana opens the driver's door and... I'm startled as her head disappears below the steering column and I'm presented with a view of her behind sticking up in the air. Not that I'm complaining.

Lana must've found what she was looking for because she straightens up and circles to the front, lifting the hood to then stare at the engine in awe.

"Isn't it beautiful?" she asks.

I come next to her and eye the double black aluminum tubes ending in a red hatch, not sure what to say. So, I guess when an engineer asks you to see the *inside* of a sports car, this is what they mean. Good to know.

"And you haven't heard it roar yet," I tell her.

Lana throws one last stare at the mechanics, then shuts the hood, saying, "Let's hear it, then."

* * *

The ride is so much more fun in the Ferrari. Lana squeaks with delight every time I speed up, and when I open the convertible roof, she tilts her face up to enjoy the sunlight's kiss on her skin.

I've never seen her so beautiful: rosy cheeks, head thrown backward, hair flying behind her in a golden-brown halo... I could stare at her for hours. Pity I have to focus on the road instead.

When we reach our destination—Griffith Observatory—thirty minutes later, it all seems too soon. We get out of the car and stop outside the iconic building to admire the Hollywood sign as the sun sets behind the mountains.

"I love this place," Lana says, leaning against the railing. "Best view in the city."

I'm glad LA has decided to help make the evening more romantic: the skies are clear, and even the usual pall of smog has magically lifted, leaving us with an unobstructed view all the way to the ocean.

We kiss and enjoy the panorama a little longer, until Lana asks, "So, what's the plan?"

"Dinner first, and then I'll show you your present."

I need the sky to be completely dark before I do.

"Dinner, here?" She looks around, perplexed. "Hey, it's quiet today. Usually, the lawns are full of people."

"Err... they might be closed to the public on Mondays."

"Might, huh?" Lana is smiling in a pretend-reproachful way.

"And I may or may have not rented the entire place for us."

Lana keeps the same mock-scolding expression. "And all for under a hundred dollars. What a deal."

"Okay, location costs were not factored into the budget, but I promise your present is dirt cheap."

"Did anyone ever tell you what a charmer you are?"

Laughing, we head toward the entrance, where an attendant is already waiting for us. I asked for the dinner table to be set outside on the upper terrace, and I'm very pleased with the result. The setting couldn't be any more romantic.

No wonder Richard proposed here, and no wonder Blair said yes. My best friend is a lucky man. And even if I'm not proposing tonight, I'm still super nervous. Maybe because Lana was so tense earlier and, for the first time, she seemed overwhelmed by my life-style—by our relationship.

But, as the date progresses, Lana visibly relaxes. I charm the tension of the weekend scandal and bag debacle out of her, mercilessly flirting until she goes back to being the smiling, carefree woman I love.

Did I say love?

Yep.

Because I do love her. Lana made me fall harder and faster than a teenage boy with his first crush.

Should I tell her now?

Better to wait until the real kick of the evening, which comes after dinner.

Once we're done eating, a volunteer—a tall, gangly man in his forties with a scholarly look—gives us a private tour of the observatory. The visit, as per my request, ends at one of the high-precision telescopes. There, he lectures us about the star systems and the galaxies for a good half hour, until finally, he gets to the good part.

The man positions the telescope at a particular angle, and says, "Now, Lana, if you could look through the lens, I'd like to show you something special."

Lana obliges him and presses her eye close to the small viewing circle. "What am I searching for?"

"You see the star resting in the center of the constellation? The one sitting a little further apart from the others?"

"Yeah, I think so," Lana says, eyes still glued to the lenses. "Why?"

"I present to you: the Christiana."

"The what?" Lana straightens up, looking perplexed. Then she catches my gaze and beams brighter than any star I've ever seen. "You bought me a star?" she asks.

"Yes," I say. "I named it for us."

Lana throws her arms around my neck and gives me a quick peck on the lips. "It's the best present ever. I love it."

I love you, I think. But still, I don't say the words out loud. To declare for the first time in front of Mr. Gangly here would be awful. Or, at least, that's what I tell myself.

Why is it taking me so damn long to express my feelings?

Probably because the last person I gave my heart to crushed it without mercy. Or maybe I'm just scared Lana isn't there yet.

So, instead, I pull her close into a—*wordless*—kiss.

The volunteer tut-tuts behind us, prompting us to break apart, and informs us the tour is over and that we must leave the premises in half an hour. We thank him, say goodbye, and take turns looking through the telescope.

"She's beautiful," Lana says, referring to the Christiana. "How will I find her again after tonight?"

I pull the certificate with the celestial address of the star and its constellation out of my jacket.

"Here are the coordinates," I say. "And if you download the app, it'll show you where the star is, no matter where in the world you are."

After more stargazing and kissing, our time at the observatory runs out and we're forced to leave.

Lana stops next to the Ferrari instead of immediately getting in. I go to her, and she gathers both my hands in hers, saying, "Thank you for tonight. It's been magical."

I read the unspoken message in her blue eyes: *"Thank you for turning a crap birthday into a beautiful evening."*

As we get into the car and leave for home, I feel like I'm flying.

26

CHRISTIAN

Fly too high, and you'll burn.

On the drive home, I avoid the shorter but more crowded route through Sunset Boulevard and take the long way up and around the park. But halfway down the hill on Coldwater Canyon Avenue, I notice a black sedan in the rearview mirror getting suspiciously close. I speed up to test my hunch, and the car matches my acceleration, keeping right on our tail.

I curse under my breath.

"Is something wrong?" Lana asks.

"Paps, following us."

She turns back to stare at the sedan just as the idiot driving, in a reckless maneuver, pulls up next to us, invading the adjoining lane. The man in the passenger seat snaps a series of photos in quick succession, and they fall back again.

I'm half-blinded by the repeated flashes, but I keep my eyes on the road, pushing down on the gas to lose the paparazzi. Their ride is no match for the Ferrari. And I didn't have the head pilot of Scuderia Ferrari show me how their cars should be handled at last year's Grand Prix in Austin for nothing. I should be able to shake the paps off quickly.

"Christian," Lana says, "you're going too fast."

"I'm trying to get rid of them."

I cut a turn at a sharp angle and Lana grabs at the passenger door in fear.

"Slow down!" she half-screams.

"I can't," I say, checking the rearview mirror. The sedan is losing ground, but its headlights are still visible. "The paps are still behind us."

"I don't care," Lana says, agitated. "You're driving too fast. Slow down."

"I don't like it when they ambush me like that—"

"And I don't like you driving *way* over the speed limit. Who cares if they take our picture! Let them. Christian, you're scaring me."

A quick glance at the gauges on the dashboard confirms Lana is right; I'm well over the limit. But with the Ferrari, all it takes is a small push. I still want to lose those bastards, but the pleading note in Lana's voice makes me lift my foot from the gas. Scaring her is something I never want to do.

She breathes a sigh of relief as the Ferrari loses momentum, and I take the next turn nice and easy.

Headlights appear in my rearview mirror, getting too close too fast. Those idiots are still racing to catch up with us.

Are they going to slow down, or what?

But those lights keep on growing bigger and brighter until they seem to be bearing right into us.

A fraction of a second passes from the moment I realize they're going to hit us and when they do, crashing the hood of their sedan against the rear end of the Ferrari.

I lose control of the wheel, and we're pushed off the side of the road. I try to steer the car back up, without success, and our skid only ends when we crash head-first into a tree.

I blink, opening my eyes, and for a moment I don't know where I am or what happened. My neck hurts, everything hurts, and there's a giant white balloon in my face. I try to straighten up, but something holds me firmly in place... *A seat belt.*

And this thing in my face must be *the airbag.*

Lana!

"Lana," I call aloud, struggling to get the white fabric out of the way. "Are you okay?"

She moans next to me.

With the airbag taking up so much space, I can't see anything, and it's impossible to reach across to Lana to check on her.

In a panic, I unbuckle the seat belt and struggle with the car door to shove it open. I push, push, and push until it gives way, and I tumble out of the seat, collapsing to my knees on the ground. I take two deep breaths of fresh air and then, on unsteady legs, I circle around the car to reach Lana.

The front of the Ferrari is hugging a tree, the metal of the hood all crumpled like the red aluminum foil of a crushed Coke can. The only illumination comes from the car's headlights that, miraculously, are still working. But the dense steam cloud coming off the engine doesn't allow me to see through the windshield.

I need to get Lana out. I hurry around the tree to her side.

The passenger door is stuck as well; I fight with it until it gives way and tears open.

"Lana," I repeat. "Can you hear me?"

I push the passenger airbag back, away from her face.

She opens her beautiful eyes and stares at me in confusion for a few long seconds.

"What happened?" she asks.

She's conscious. A breath of relief I didn't know I'd been holding since I came to my senses leaves my lungs.

"We were in an accident," I say. "Are you okay?"

I watch her turn her neck and wince in pain. "I think so."

"Can you move? Can you get out of the car?"

Lana nods, so I unbuckle the seat belt for her and help her out of the seat.

She takes a few wobbly steps, holding on to my arms for support.

"Are you hurt?" I ask.

"No, nothing serious." Then her gaze turns to the edge of the cliff the tree stopped us from tumbling down to. Had we gone over, we could've died. "What about the other car; are they okay?"

Give it to Lana to worry about others first.

Looking up, I'm blinded by the sedan's headlights. "Looks like they stopped on the road." As opposed to us; we skidded a few yards down the slope until the tree blocked our descent.

"Good," Lana says. "Good."

She begins trembling in my arms, her wide, panicked eyes searching the night.

"Good," she repeats. "Good."

The last one comes out in half a sob. My chest tightens at seeing her like this. I try to pull her to me to stop her shaking, but she resists me.

"I can't," she says, taking a few steps backward and stumbling on the underbrush.

Her chest starts heaving, and the trembling worsens.

All the signs are there: she's having a panic attack.

"It's okay," I try to reassure her. "You're in shock. It'll pass."

"No." She keeps shaking her head. "I can't."

"Lana, let's get back to the road. You need to sit down. Everything will be all right."

"No, it won't." She stares both at the crashed Ferrari and at the wreck of the Sedan. "This life," she says, still breathing heavily. "It's too much. I-I can't do it."

"Lana, I get it. You're scared, but nothing happened, really."

"Nothing?" she repeats, glaring at me. "A car chased us off the road..." More heavy breaths. "We're standing in a ditch an inch away from a several-foot drop, alive by a miracle. We could've died!"

"But we didn't. No one got hurt." I take a step toward her. "We're fine."

"I'm not fine!" she yells. So I stop. "I don't know how you do it." Her hair is wild, sticking out in all directions, and she's flapping her arms like a crazy person. "The constant scrutiny," she continues, "people following you everywhere you go, everyone asking for a piece of you... *always*. It's relentless. I'm not cut out for this."

"It was just two idiots trying to make a few quick bucks. I can't control them."

"But you can control how you drive," Lana fires right back. "The paparazzi wouldn't have gone so fast if you didn't try to lose them."

"Okay, I made a mistake," I say, even if I don't really think what happened here tonight is in any way my fault. "It won't happen again."

"How can you be so sure?" Lana leans against a tree for support. "You said you can't control what happens."

"Like no one can. Car accidents happen every day—"

"Not to me." She coughs. "I don't drive, and especially not in fast sports cars. And I don't have to run away from every moron with a camera who wants to take my picture. I should be concentrating on salvaging what's left of my career. Not waste time going to movie premiers, or running away from rough paparazzi, or wasting brainpower worrying about what my ex is going to sell to the press next."

"What do you want me to say? I can't change who I am."

"No, you can't," Lana says, her voice carrying a ring of steel. "But neither can I."

It's not the hardness in her tone that punches me right in the solar plexus, but the deep sorrow in her eyes. That's the look of someone saying goodbye.

"You're shaken," I say, trying to scale back the fight. "We need to burn off the adrenaline. I'll call Penny, she can come to pick us up, and we can discuss everything at home."

"I can't come with you," she says, confirming my fears. "Sorry." Lana breaks out in heavy sobs. "I can't do this. This life... it's not for me." She seems to make the realization as she speaks, as if even she is caught by surprise. Eyes wider still, she looks up at me and says, "I'm sorry, I can't be with you."

"Lana, don't say this," I plead. "You're overreacting."

"And you're not listening," she says as tears roll down her cheeks. "I'm a quiet person. I love my reserved life, working on my research, teaching my students, reading a novel in my free time... and my idea of an adventure is to hike a new trail in the hills. This" —Lana does a swipe of her arms toward the crashed Ferrari— "this is not me. I tried to pretend it didn't matter, that I was fine with it because I—"

She suddenly stops.

"Because you...?"

Lana shakes her head.

"What were you about to say?"

We're interrupted by a bright flash slashing through the night.

Oh, that scumbag didn't *dare*.

I'm so worked up by the accident and the fight with Lana that I climb out of the ditch, march toward the dude, and snatch the camera from his hands. I smash it to the ground and kick it away in a rage.

"Hey, you can't do that," the sleazebag dares to complain.

"I can do whatever the hell I want. In case you didn't notice, you ran us down with your car..."

"Oh, you what? Broke one of your favorite toys," the guy says.

"You could've killed us, you idiot."

"Whoa, killed? No one got hurt. You actors really have a flair for drama."

I grab him by the collar of his shirt, and I don't know what I'm about to do when Lana stops me, yelling, "Christian, don't!"

It's the anguish in her voice that makes all the fight drain out of me. I let the guy go and turn toward her.

Lana raises her hands, putting them between us like a barrier. "Don't," she says. "I'm texting Marjory. See if she can come to pick me up."

"Okay," I say, trying to keep as calm as I can. "It's good. Stay with a friend tonight. We can talk again tomorrow when we're both calmer."

"No." One word, pronounced in a half sob, is enough to shatter my heart into a million pieces. "I can't... I can't see you anymore. S-sorry. I can't live like this."

The truth of that last sentence breaks through the veil of my denial and makes me go limp.

Dating me, she'd hate every minute of this life. Hollywood would chew her up and spit her out in a blink. Acting has always been my dream, and sometimes, even I can't stand all that comes attached to being famous. Even after years of growing a thick skin. How can I ask the same of Lana? It wouldn't be fair.

Nothing about tonight is fair.

I want to hug Lana, to kiss her one last time, but if I do, I won't be able to let her go. So I only nod and go sit by the side of the road.

The following silence is broken by police sirens, joined closely by an ambulance. Two cops take our statements and the paramedics do a check on us. And I get little pleasure in seeing the two idiots who just ruined my life handcuffed and loaded in the back seat of the police car. Two paps getting charged for reckless endangerment won't solve a damn thing.

By the time the officers and paramedics are done, Lana's friend has arrived, too.

Lana murmurs something to the woman, who nods and goes to wait in her car. Then Lana walks toward me. With tears in her eyes, she rises on the tips of her toes, plants a soft kiss on my cheek, and whispers, "I'm sorry."

I inhale the scent of her hair one last time, then stand there and watch her leave, taking the pieces of my broken heart with her.

* * *

"The Ferrari is beyond repair," Penny informs me the next morning. "Would cost more to fix than to buy a new one."

I'm up earlier than usual after spending a sleepless night tossing in bed. Dawn has barely broken, and I'm already sitting in my office with Penny, managing the fallout from the accident.

"The insurance will cover the residual value," my assistant continues. "But to be made whole, you'll have to sue the two bastards who ran you off the road."

I click a pen compulsively to keep my hands busy. "No."

"No, what?"

"I'm not going to sue."

"Why not? They—"

"I'll let the police deal with them. The cops have my statement."

"So the paps walk?"

"They'll get whatever punishment our justice system deems fair. But I don't need to go after them for money. I don't give a damn"—I smash a fist on my desk—"about a few extra bucks or a broken car."

The pen in my hand snaps.

I hold Penny's widened gaze, and I can read in her expression she gets what I really mean: the only thing I cared about is gone.

I look away, wishing my assistant couldn't read me so well. A pity party is the last thing I need today.

"Actually, have the legal team threaten them with a lawsuit anyway," I say.

"Because...?"

"They need to scare them into signing a non-disclose. I don't want a peep about last night in the press."

"Might be already too late for that," Penny informs me. "A short article came out on TMZ."

"We need to get ahead of it, release a statement," I say. "Make it clear the accident was just that, an accident. No DUI, no reckless driving. You can say I was trying to avoid a raccoon and lost control of the car, or something. Whatever makes sense, but leave Lana and the paparazzi out of the story."

Just saying her name is too painful.

How am I going to get past her?

Focus, Christian, you'll deal with your broken heart later.

Now you owe Lana her life back.

Penny notes everything I want to be done and then stares at me expectantly in an *anything-else* way.

So I brace myself for what I have to do next. "One last thing..."

27

LANA

The next morning, I wake up in a raging panic. Not about the accident, I realize. Even if nightmares of strangers following me and pushing me into bottomless holes have haunted me all night.

In the light of day, I'm more worried I made the worst call of my life yesterday.

Pushing Christian away was a mistake.

What was I thinking?

I blamed him for the accident when it wasn't his fault those two idiots chasing us didn't know how to drive. And then I panicked and blamed him some more for... *everything*, basically.

And then I broke up with him.

A crack spreads across my heart. Oh, gosh, is this what real heartbreak feels like? The mere possibility of never seeing Christian again is making my chest pull tight; a black hole has taken the place of my heart, absorbing every happy feeling I've ever had and destroying them. And the sensation terrifies me more than any car accident ever could.

I make to grab my phone and call him when I see the time on the screen.

Shoot, I'm late.

I overslept.

Did I miss the alarm?

It doesn't matter; I have to be in class in less than half an hour.

I jump out of bed, ignoring the lingering soreness from the seat belt whiplash, and get dressed at the speed of light. I feed the cats and borrow Winter's car to get to campus on time. She left me the Prius keys to use while she's away.

I'll call Christian once the lecture is over.

* * *

"...And that's all for today's class," I say three seemingly endless hours later. "Are there any questions?"

I scan the lecture hall, but no hands lift up.

"Good, class dismissed," I announce. "Remember to drop off your homework before you leave. See you on Friday."

I wait seated behind my desk for each student to deliver their homework and file out. The last one to leave is a shy Asian student with a mind as sharp as a knife.

She drops her paper on top of the others and eyes me in an odd way.

"Can I help you with anything, Kim?" I ask.

"No." She shakes her head sadly. "Just wanted to say I'm sorry."

I frown, confused. "For what?"

"I saw the announcement on celebritygossip.com," she says, eyes full of pity. "Guess no matter how good they look on paper, men are all the same."

I don't know how to reply, so I only thank her, while a horrible sense of foreboding settles in my guts.

Once I'm alone in the lecture hall, I grab my phone and, with shaky fingers, type "celebritygossip.com" into the web browser.

There it is, the first article on the homepage. The headline slashes through my heart like a blade:

OLIVIA THORNTON CONFIRMS SHE'S DATING CHRISTIAN SLADE, SAYS THEY'RE IN LOVE
OLIVIA THORNTON CHRISTIAN SLADE RUMORS ARE TRUE... WE'RE DATING AND IN LOVE!!!

I read on, my pulse speeding up to an unhealthy pumping.

Slade and Thornton were spotted having breakfast in the Hollywood Hills earlier this morning. Only one reason, folks, why the two of them would be sharing a PDA-packed meal at such an early hour.
A sweet treat after a night of passion?
Upon being later approached, it didn't take much prodding before Thornton confirmed it was true and began gushing over her man, calling him an amazing human being and saying their relationship is a wonderful thing.
She continued... "I am grateful to be with someone that I value and love and admire so much," and added several more doting words to describe her professional and personal respect for fellow actor Slade.

Below the article, there's a picture of Christian in sweatpants and a T-shirt kissing an equally casually dressed and unbelievably beautiful woman. The caption reads:

OLIVIA THORNTON BESAME MUCHO!!!
Locks Lips w/ British Bae

My stomach turns. *How can this be?* Christian and I were together only last night. Has he found a new girlfriend two seconds after breaking up with me? I can't believe this. As I finish reading the article, I tell myself there must be another explanation.

BTW... it appears Christian has moved on from his last fling... with UCLA rocket scientist Miss Nobody. They went public only last month at the movie premiere of Christian's latest box office smashing success, but his smooch with Olivia seems to signify Christian's previous relationship has gone kaput.

As for whether wedding bells are on the horizon for Olivia and Christian... she's not quite ready to say.

I honestly have no idea what to think. This all seems pretty absurd. I've seen firsthand what lies the gossip machine can spur. No way Christian would've gone straight to another woman last night. Slept with this Olivia person.

So what was he doing having breakfast with her and kissing her this morning?

A rebound?

No, impossible.

I should stop. I don't know when the pictures were taken, or even if they're legit.

Could the website have Photoshopped them together?

They must have.

Still, there's a seed of doubt planted in my heart now, which stops me from calling Christian right away. If this story is as untrue as I think it is, he'll surely release a statement rectifying the gossip. Penelope is super-efficient; she'll get a retraction out in no time.

* * *

The disclaimer is never issued. Instead, as the days pass, I'm haunted by more and more pictures of Christian and Olivia popping up everywhere I go.

Gossip magazines—items that previously lived in a total blind spot for me—are now evil entities I'm no longer able to tune out. Not when I pass by the magazine section at the bookstore. Not when I walk by a newsstand on the sidewalk. Not when I'm paying for my groceries and their colorful front pages smirk at me from the rack next to the cashier.

Christian's and Olivia's smiling, loved-up faces are always the main headline.

My only safe havens are work and my friends.

As a coping mechanism, I bury myself in my research. Double my efforts to find a new sponsor. Spectroscopy gas cells become my only partner. A pressure-controlled McKenna burner is the only thing I have physical intimacy with—except maybe for cuddles with my cats. I spend my days in the solid fuel combustion facility conducting as many experiments as humanly possible and then, even when I'm done, combing through data.

Sharing an apartment with Winter has helped immensely in feeling less lonely, and whenever she has to travel, if I don't feel like being alone, I stop at the library on the way home. Marjory has moved the magazine stand to a detached aisle so I won't have to face tabloid covers every time I enter the building.

But everywhere else I go, Christian's face follows me. It's on billboards hanging over the city, on the sides of buses, and on movie posters stuck to every wall.

How did I never notice his face before?

One day, as I'm grocery shopping, morbid curiosity wins. At the last minute before paying, I snatch a copy of the magazine with the biggest picture of Christian on the cover and buy it.

Outside, I stop to read the article.

Olivia and her new BF came up for air after hanging out Wednesday in LA. The actress was all smiles before the 32-year-old actor from England packed on some serious PDA. Olivia looked pretty biz caj... with a camel trench coat, LBD, and matching black boots. Pretty elegant, too, with an Angelika Black handbag as a statement piece.

See? She gets Angelika Black handbags. They're a perfect match. Christian can buy her tons of expensive presents and they can show off their designer clothes all over LA.

The first few lines of the article are enough to make my stomach turn, and I trash the magazine without reading the rest.

Is this how Johnathan felt when he read about Christian and me?

No, because Johnathan didn't love me, while I—what?

Love Christian?

What a fool I've been.

The deep connection I felt must've been all in my head. Christian has clearly never been serious about us. I bet for him I was a fling between one actress and the next. The weirdo who didn't know who he was, fun to date for a couple of months and then forget.

I can't stand how naïve I've been.

But the moment I hate myself the most is at night, when I step out onto Winter's small balcony, open the star-finder app, and crane my neck up to stare at the Christiana while quietly crying.

It's been three weeks, almost a month, spent following Olivia and Christian's story in pictures, and I still search the sky for our star every single night.

28

CHRISTIAN

I need out of LA. The charade has gone on long enough. I'm sick to my stomach of pretending I'm all loved up when I'm really dying inside. I couldn't continue if I wanted to.

A friend. I need my best friend.

Without alerting any of my staff, I rent a plane and jet to New York.

A different city doesn't cure my heart, but it's better to mourn sprawled on Richard's couch in his designer loft in Brooklyn than being in LA. I don't even mind lying under sixty pounds of very sympathetic dog.

Chevron, Richard's Labrador mutt, has taken my suffering to heart. With her paws and muzzle resting on my chest, she's whining emphatically and gives me the occasional comforting lick or two.

I'm busy contemplating my utter misery when I hear the key turn in the lock. I'm shielded from the door when, bringing with her a cloud of feminine perfume, Blair enters the house.

"We're late," she says, sounding agitated. There's the click-clack-click of heels hitting the concrete floor, then a swish of something heavy but soft being dropped on the ground—*her bag?*—and finally, Blair asks, "Have you set the table?"

"Hi," Richard says. "Late for what?"

"Nikki and Diego are coming for dinner. I told you a few days ago. Did you forget?"

Ah, you so did, mate.

"Was it tonight?"

From his tone, I can tell Richard has no clue.

Blair sighs. "You're lucky you have too good a bone structure for me to get mad at you."

Then I hear a smooching sound.

Mmm, hello? Have some tact; there's a recovering, brokenhearted man on your couch.

I'm sure Blair's kisses must be mind-boggling, but Richard has enough presence of mind to remember I'm here.

"Err, we have a situation," he says.

Oh, I've never been referred to as a "situation" before. Not that I know of, at least.

"What situation?" Blair asks.

"We might have one sexiest man alive nursing a heartbreak on our couch."

"Christian's here?"

More click-clack-click, and Blair's face appears over the couch. I wave at her in a hi-lovesick-man-here way.

She gives me a look. "I see you're doing some serious pet therapy there."

Blair drops her hands on the couch's backrest, and I'm almost blinded by the ginormous rock adorning her left hand.

"I can't believe you agreed to marry my rascal of a best friend," I say.

"What else could I do?" she says with a foxy grin. "The man went down on one knee and begged me."

Her sarcasm—she's always wanted to get married, while Richard had sworn he never would—makes me crack a smile.

"I'm thrilled for you," I say.

"Thank you—"

The buzzer interrupts her.

"Crap." Blair stares at her watch. "They're already here." Then she looks back down at me. "Nikki is the kind of friend I can invite to dinner and then uninvite when she's already come all the way to Brooklyn from Manhattan. If you don't want people around, she'll understand."

She throws me a *your-call* look.

"Is she cool?" I ask.

"Of course she's cool, she's my best friend," Blair says in a *duh* tone. "She may go a little fangirl on you. But I'm afraid she's bumped you to second place as the sexiest man alive after meeting her beau."

This Nikki sounds cool already, and if she has a boyfriend in tow, I don't risk any unwanted attention.

"No," I say. "It's fine. I wouldn't want to leave your friends hungry in the streets."

"Even if we're in Brooklyn, this is still New York," Blair says. "I'm sure they can find a place to eat around here."

"No, really. I'm cool."

"Okay." Blair nods, and with more click-clacking, she goes to answer the door, firing a "You set the table" at Richard.

*　*　*

Half an hour later, we're seated around the table eating something too healthy-looking for someone in my condition. But at least there's wine, and with Chevron perching on the chair next to me, I feel less of an odd number among couples.

But the conversation is a bit on the stiff side. Nikki—a pretty brunette with a short bob—and Diego—tall, dark hair, deep green eyes, and the most handsome man in the room by far—obviously didn't expect to have dinner with a celebrity. And, even if I appreciate them for trying hard to maintain a normal attitude, they're not at ease.

Time to break the oh-and-there's-an-unexpected-world-famous-guest-for-dinner ice, so to speak.

"So," I say, addressing Nikki and Diego. "How did you two guys meet?"

They exchange a look and a grin.

It's a gesture intimate enough to make my heart bleed. I could've had that with Lana...

"Oh," Diego says, still sporting half a grin. "She behaved very unprofessionally on a job last Christmas."

Nikki widens her mouth in mock outrage. "Oh, so I was the unprofessional one?"

He winks at her. "You were the boss; you took advantage."

There's clearly more of a story there, something perhaps they're not comfortable discussing with a complete stranger. So I move on to the next obvious—and hopefully less painful to witness—topic.

"What do you guys do?" And with a cheeky grin, I add, "I'm in entertainment."

Nikki laughs, then answers, "Advertising, at an agency on Madison Avenue. We specialize in video commercials. I'm a producer."

I turn to Diego next.

He shifts in his chair, clearly uncomfortable. "Man, I feel really awkward saying this in front of you... but I'm an actor."

Oh, yeah, that was definitely unexpected. I brace myself for the customary follow-up entreaties: Can you give me your agent's number? Can you introduce me to your producers/directors/movie friends? Can you... whatever else for me?

But Diego only gives me a lopsided, awkward-I-know grin, and I immediately like the guy a hundred times better.

"Have I seen you in something?" I ask. Now that I take a better look at him, he seems familiar but... *wrong*, somehow. Like he was wearing the wrong clothes or hair.

And then I get a flash of galloping horses and Nordic warriors. "Wait, you were the Viking king in that Super Bowl commercial!" I superimpose on him the braided long hair and beard and imagine him riding on horseback in full armor. Definitely him. "That ad had me cracking up."

Diego nods and smiles. "Flattered you remembered, man."

I nod back. "Are you working on something else at the moment?"

"Snatched my first real part on Broadway." Diego's smile is proud this time. "Only a supporting role, but the cast is stellar and my name is on the manifest, so I can't complain."

"What's the play?"

Diego swallows a bite before answering, "*Trudy and Truman.* It's a fun act. You should come see it."

I become wary again, thinking the help-me-get-where-you-are request will arrive after all.

But Diego only says, "We're sold out for the season, but I can get you a ticket if you'd like."

Damn, I like this guy. "Yeah, sure, mate, that'd be great."

"So, what brings you to New York?" Nikki asks.

Ah, I wanted the conversation to get flowing... and now it comes back to bite me in the arse.

I take a sip of wine and make the liquid swirl in the glass. "Only the oldest story in the book: a man, a woman, and a broken heart."

Nikki's smile drops. "Oh, I'm sorry. Did you and Olivia break up?"

I grimace bitterly. Well, at least I have confirmation my ruse worked.

Before replying, I turn to Blair, hesitant.

"You're off the record and among friends," she quickly reassures me. "You can trust everyone in this room to keep this conversation private. Nothing you say will be repeated outside these walls." Then, with a crooked smile, she adds, "I can make them all do the scout salute if it makes you feel better."

I grin back. "No need." Then I turn back to Nikki. "The relationship with Olivia was fake; a business arrangement."

Blair's friend looks more confused than ever, so I tell them about Lana, our relationship, her dislike of public attention, and about the night of the crash. "The only way to get the press off her back was to feed them another, juicier story, so that's what I did. I asked my assistant to find me a down-to-business actress interested in some extra publicity, and Olivia was the perfect match. She eagerly agreed to play along."

The table remains in stunned silence for a few seconds, until Blair says, "So, let me get this straight. You're still 100 percent in love with Lana, but instead of trying to win her back, you made the entire world—*including her*—believe you're dating someone else?"

I shift the green and brown food around my plate with my fork. "Lana wanted the paparazzi off her back. I gave her what she asked for."

Blair and Nikki exchange a *poor bastard* look.

"Are you sure there's no way to win your woman back?" Diego asks. Then, with another small grin meant for Nikki alone, he adds, "Even desperate situations can turn out for the best if you try hard enough."

"Lana was clear: she wanted nothing to do with me and my lifestyle."

"But you guys had just been in an accident," Blair says. "Maybe she was in shock, or scared, and that was something she said in the heat of the moment. Did you give her time to reconsider?"

"Err..."

"How long after the accident did you have the Olivia lie circulate?" Blair presses.

"The next morning?"

The female audience gasps—Chevron included.

"So you buy this woman a star," Nikki says, utterly appalled, "and the next day you splash a fake rebound hook-up on her?"

"Only to get the press off her back," I insist.

"Yeah, mate," Richard chimes in. "But is there any way Lana could've known it was a fake story?"

"There's no way she'd believe I could be with someone else so soon. She knows me better than that. And she doesn't read gossip magazines, anyway."

"But some of her friends might, or her family," Nikki says.

"And it wasn't a one-off," Blair adds. "You kept the story going for weeks." She blushes. "Sorry, celebrity gossip is my jam."

"So what should I have done?" I ask.

They all give their two pence:

Blair. "Given Lana a chance to process."

Chevron. *"Woof."*

Richard. "Begged her to take you back."

Diego. "Gotten her a kitten."

Nikki mock-scolds her boyfriend at what is clearly another inside joke, then says, "Told the woman you love her."

I start at that.

"You did tell her you're in love with her, didn't you?" Nikki insists. "At least once, right?"

"Mmm, I might have implied it with my actions...?"

Blair attacks next. "But you didn't say the actual words?"

"No, I didn't. I couldn't seem to find the right time."

"How much do you love her?" Nikki asks.

"Is there a scale?" I ask, perplexed.

Nikki and Blair exchange a nod, and Blair talks next. "If she suffered from short-term amnesia and forgot you every night as she went to sleep, would you make her fall in love with you all over again every day?"

I'm taken aback by the question. "What?"

"Just answer them, mate," Richard suggests. "They have this annoying habit of comparing every real-life situation to movies."

"What movie is that again?"

"50 First Dates," Blair and Nikki reply at once.

I sigh. "I guess I would?"

"Woof, woof," Chevron interjects. Blair translates for her: "She's probably asking if you'd share spaghetti and meatballs with Lana. Chevron loves watching *Lady and the Tramp*."

"I would," I say, more definitively this time.

"Woof," Chevron approves.

The next question comes from Nikki. "Would you run after her in the snow, wearing only 'genuinely tiny knickers'?"

Oh, I know this one. *Bridget Jones.*

"Are the tiny knickers a requirement?"

"Definitely," she says.

"Then yes."

Richard shakes his head, amused.

"Now, the final test," Blair continues, unfazed. "Your ship has sunk in the freezing Northern Atlantic Ocean and there's only a plank of driftwood to hold on to, but it can only fit one of you. Would you—"

"Yeah, she can have the damn plank," I interrupt. And so help me, I mean every word of it.

"Then it is true love," Blair says. "You can't give up and accept it's over."

I drop the fork and stop pretending I'm eating. "Sorry, but it's not up to me."

"If you give up you've still made a choice," Blair insists. "What do you have to lose in trying, anyway?"

"Well, having my heart walked all over *twice* wouldn't exactly be fun."

"Neither is being a moping grouch," Nikki says. "Respectfully."

"*Woof.*"

"What if Lana doesn't want to talk to me?" I ask. "What if she believed the Olivia story? I'd hate my guts if I were her."

"Then be creative," Blair says as she gets up and starts collecting plates. "Force her to listen."

"*Woof.*"

"All right, ladies, you win. I'll think of something."

"Here, mate." Richard pours me more wine.

I raise my glass and say, "To the great romantic gesture."

29

CHRISTIAN

New day. Time for a new plan.

After sharing the sofa bed with Chevron, I wake up galvanized. With a purpose. I still don't know what I'm going to do. But a tiny seed of hope to win Lana back is enough to make me feel a thousand times better than I have these past few weeks.

Richard and Blair have already left for work, so I'm alone in their house. I don my standard, public-spaces disguise—baseball cap, hoodie, sunglasses—and head outside. If I met myself in a dark alley, I'd think I was about to get mugged. But the gangster look is the only style that allows me to walk the streets undetected.

Last night, Diego gave me a ticket to a matinee showing of his play, so I take a cab to Broadway to watch it. Immersing myself in the creative arts is the best way to find inspiration.

I haven't been to the theater in too long. Hollywood makes it so easy to forget the beauty of performing in front of a real audience. And the live show leaves me even more energized; the plot is original and witty, and Diego is a stellar actor.

As the curtains close, I'm tempted to go behind the scenes to congratulate him, but I don't want to attract any unnecessary attention. I exit the theater instead and walk all the way to Central Park, enjoying the indifference of the New York crowds.

In LA, every tourist, and even some natives, are all on a constant celebrity hunt. Here, everyone seems to mind their own business. Vacationers are more interested in the architecture than in noticing who's walking beside them.

Blissfully ignored by passers-by, I buy a hot dog from one of the famous street carts and go eat it on a bench in the park.

So, Lana. How do I convince you to give me a second chance?

I flashback to the time we've spent together, from the night at the observatory backward to the day we met in the Peninsula's closet.

And then it hits me. The perfect solution.

I take out my phone and call my assistant.

Penny picks up on the first ring. "Sometimes they return," she says.

"Hi," I say. "Listen—"

"No, please, feel free to go MIA on me whenever you want," she scolds. "It's so much fun to deal with all the people you've stood up, blowing up my phone asking where you are, why you left, when you're coming back—"

"Sorry! I needed a break."

Penny sighs. "*Men,* always using the 'on a break' excuse. So what can I do for you, boss?"

"Remember that sci-fi flick Marvin wanted me to do so badly last March?"

"Yeah?"

"Have they already offered the lead to someone else?"

"I don't know, but I can call Samantha Baker and find out."

"Please do, and call me back ASAP."

* * *

Two days later, I've made my agent a very happy man by signing the contract with Denouement Studios to be the lead in their blockbuster movie *The Descendant of Dawn*. The studio was so desperate to hire me, I managed to make them agree to all my unconventional requests—more shooting time in LA, filming must start right away, a generous donation to a cause close to my heart, and the hiring of a script consultant of my choosing.

The lead producer for this project, Samantha Baker, is based here in Denouement's New York branch. So I kill two birds with one stone and attend a pre-production meeting with the movie team that has been scheduled to introduce me to the rest of the cast and crew.

The meeting is taking place in a swanky glass room high above in a skyscraper in central Manhattan. There are a lot of friendly faces here. The director is a good friend of mine, and we've worked together in the past. I also know some of the cast members— mostly attending via video conference. And Samantha is one of my favorite producers to work with; I've done several movies with her.

She has given the team a rundown of the project: from schedule, to location, costumes, photography, special effects, and the training each actor will have to undertake for his/her specific role. Seems I must learn lightsaber fighting.

"This leaves us with only one major point unsolved," Samantha says, as she nears the conclusion of her presentation. "The casting of Morrigan."

Morrigan is the evil overlord from a destitute planet who wants to subjugate the entire galaxy.

"Christian joining the cast as our hero is wonderful news," Samantha continues, nodding toward me. "But if we want this movie to be a success, we have to find a great villain, too. Unfortunately, I had confirmation last night that Jason Pratt officially turned down the role."

And thank goodness, I think.

The guy's a self-absorbed, arrogant prick with a huge ego, and he's a nightmare to work with. Six foot five of muscles with no brain.

"We've looked at several other candidates, but with no luck so far." Samantha pulls a lock of her super-straight-above-the-shoulders bob behind her ear. "We need someone exceptionally tall for the role, especially now that Christian has come on board. And as you know, that's not an easy find."

An idea pops into my head.

"Hey," I say. "Would you consider an unknown actor?"

"If he was good and fit the physical description, why not?" Samantha says.

"I have the perfect guy for you."

I grab my phone and google Diego's Super Bowl ad. He looks mighty fierce as a Viking king and perfect for the part of the villain in our story.

I hand the phone to Samantha and she watches the short commercial.

"Mmm," she says once it's over.

I would've expected a little more enthusiasm.

"What do you think?" I prompt.

"The guy's really handsome," Samantha says, with a downward curve of her mouth.

"Oh, is that a bad thing? I didn't see 'must be ugly' in the physical description."

"True." She hands me back the phone. "But this guy is *exceptionally* good-looking."

"And that's a problem because...?"

"In our experience, having two very handsome leads can foster conflicts on set."

I frown.

"You know, big personalities and all..." Samantha trails off.

And the shoe drops. "Are you calling me a prima donna?"

"No, I'm saying that if you put this guy on screen, he might very well end up as the Sexiest Man Alive next year."

"Ah, hell, they can't name me every single year, now, can they?"

"So you wouldn't have a problem in sharing the female fandom?"

"No."

Samantha finally cracks a smile. "Then, yes, he'd be perfect. Guys," she addresses the room. "That's all for today. We re-adjourn in a week."

While the others leave, Samantha gestures for me to stay behind.

"I'm so glad Marvin convinced you to sign. This part was made for you."

"You could've sweet-talked me into it yourself," I say. "Long time no see in LA."

"Oh." She brushes me off with a perfectly-manicured hand. "You know how I am; take me out of New York and I wither."

I take in her pale skin. "Not a sunshine lover?"

"Nah, I'm more of an indoor gal. So, this guy," she says, going straight back to business. "Where did you find him?"

"He was at dinner at a friend's house the other night."

"And how do you know he's a good actor?" Samantha sounds skeptical again. "I mean, he's a magnificent horse rider, but other than that?"

"I went to see him on Broadway the other day; he has a supporting role in *Trudy and Truman*."

"Oh, I've heard great things about that show."

"Go watch it, see for yourself."

"This guy owes you a real solid. How come you're going out on a limb for him?"

I give her the simple, honest truth. "Because he didn't ask."

* * *

Apparently, all the private jets in New York are rented; I couldn't find even a biplane to take me back to LA with a few hours' notice.

A disaster. I haven't flown commercially in years, and the prospect scares me. Gangster look or not, there's always the risk of people recognizing me. Still, if I want to get back to LA tonight, I have no choice.

I say goodbye to Richard and Blair, and almost steal Chevron, before I go catch the red-eye flight to Los Angeles. I'm going to miss that pup.

Before leaving, I didn't tell my friends about Diego and the movie in case nothing comes of it. I wouldn't want to get his hopes up and then crush them. But I'm sure that if Samantha goes to see the play, she'll offer him the part on the spot.

When I get to JFK, the airport is almost empty. So, instead of hiding in the first-class lounge, I take my chances at a regular bar near the departure board.

Even though the place is deserted, I still take a seat at the far-end corner of the counter. Old habits.

The barman—younger than me, with short sandy hair, a broad smile, and a friendly face—immediately comes to serve his only customer.

"What can I get you?"

"A beer, please," I say, looking up at him.

I had to remove the sunglasses, as wearing them indoors would've been more conspicuous than keeping them off.

The bartender and I make eye contact, and I wait for his eyes to widen in recognition. They don't.

"Lager, or something stronger?"

"Do you have Guinness?"

"Sure." He walks back to the fridge and takes out a can of Guinness.

While he's pouring the beer into a glass, two other customers arrive. Is it my imagination, or did the dude move the potato chips rack to shield me from their view? Intentional or not, I'm glad for the makeshift screen.

Turns out it wasn't necessary. The couple only buy a bottle of water and then hurry away. *Phew.*

I'm sipping my beer and waiting for the boarding announcement for my plane when the bartender comes back over to check on me. I turn down his offer of another beer. Then he asks me, "Enjoyed your visit to New York?"

Ah, so he's the talker type. *Wonderful.*

"How do you know I'm not from here and taking a trip now?" I ask.

"Slightly too healthy, natural tan to live in the city."

True. I feel weird answering questions from strangers, so I give him a vague answer. "It was only a short trip, visiting friends."

"I can tell New York has worked its magic on you," the guy says, surprising me.

"How do you mean?"

"You have that look of someone who came to the Big Apple lost and is going back with a newfound purpose."

Uncommon sixth sense, indeed. I neither confirm nor deny his observation. I only shrug.

The bartender takes the hint I'm not in the mood to talk and goes back to unloading glasses from the dishwasher and putting them onto the shelves.

We don't talk again until it's time for me to leave and pay the bill. I walk up to the cash register and give the bartender my credit card.

He processes the payment, then hesitates. "Man," he says. "You probably hate this, but can I ask you for an autograph for my sister? She'd haunt me to my grave if she knew you'd passed through my bar and I didn't ask."

This guy almost had me fooled; I truly believed he hadn't recognized me. "Did you know who I was the entire time?"

"I wasn't sure until I saw it in writing." He flips my credit card, showing me the name part, before giving it back.

I smile. Makes sense. "What's your sister's name?"

"Gwen. Gwen Cooper. I'm Mark."

"Hi, Mark." I grab a napkin. "You have a pen?"

He gives me one, and I write my standard short dedication.

When I'm done, the bartender takes the napkin and shifts on his feet, clearly torn. I've been at this game long enough to get his dilemma. It usually annoys me, but I like this guy even if I don't know him, so I say, "You have a mother, too? Girlfriend, aunt, best friend? Which one is it?"

"Mother," he says with a goofy smile. "Margaret."

I pen a replica napkin for the mom and give it to him.

"Thank you, man," Mark says. "Have a safe trip home."

I touch two fingers to my forehead in farewell and head to the gate.

Thankfully, my seat in first class is next to a businessman who doesn't look like someone who has much time to watch movies. So I lower the back seat, pull a sleeping mask over my eyes, and wake up only when we touch ground in LAX.

I have no luggage besides my carry-on, so I make a quick exit. The warm LA air and Bill are waiting for me outside—no paps. My driver loads my small suitcase into the trunk, and I hop in the car, riding shotgun as he drives me home. I've never been a believer in the driver-in-the-front, passenger-in-the-back riding style.

As we zip through the streets of LA, I stare up at the sky through the side window, searching for the Christiana. But without the app—I saw no point in downloading it after what happened as it would've only been a knife in the open wound of my heart—I have no clue where her constellation is. I wonder what Lana is doing right now. Is she looking at the skies, seeking the same star? Our star?

My stomach flutters at the thought that I'll see her again soon. I only have to hope my plan to win her back will work... *What good is being the sexiest man alive if I can't have the only woman I want?*

30

LANA

I'm noting down the results of my latest time-resolved thrust profile measurements test, when someone taps me on the shoulder.

I turn to find Trevor standing behind me.

He looks at me with a slightly apologetic face. "Sorry to interrupt."

Aware I've gone a little maniac at work lately and barked at people for a lot less, I school my features into their most polite expression. "No worries, what's up?"

"I come from Conway's office; he's asked me to send you there."

"What, right now?"

"Yes, it sounded urgent."

"Okay." I check my watch. "I'll finish collecting the thermo-chemistry measurements and I'll go."

"I can do it for you if you want."

I don't like to pawn off my work on others, but if Conway wants to see me urgently in his office it could be about my grant. Piloto, a company I've been in talks with, could've made an official offer.

I hand Trevor my notepad. "Thank you, I owe you one."

"No problem."

I leave him in the lab and hurry toward Dr. Conway's office.

"Ah, Lana," my adviser welcomes me. "Come in. I have wonderful news to share. Please take a seat." He gestures to the empty chair in front of his desk.

My heart pounds as my best hopes are confirmed, Piloto must've made an offer.

My adviser crosses his hands over the desk and announces, "I'm happy to inform you that an official grant offer has come through that would cover your entire fellowship for the next academic year."

Even if I was expecting it, my jaw drops. With relief mostly. "Is it from Piloto?"

"Not quite, not quite. Rather unexpected, or"—he gives me an unreadable look— "maybe not so much unexpected, given—" He stops mid-sentence and starts again. "But let's not focus on the details. The important thing is that your funding is secured, right?"

"Right," I agree.

"So you wouldn't mind if the donation came with a small condition attached to it."

The man is being suspiciously casual, so I ask, "What condition?"

"The donor has requested you for a consultancy."

"Who's the donor?" I ask, even more on alert.

"Denouement Studios," Dr. Conway says. "They're filming some sort of space opera movie, and they've requested the university's collaboration to make sure all the physics and space travel in the film are more or less realistic."

My heart sinks and jumps at the same time, if that's possible. I flashback to the first night I met Christian when I stood on the doorstep and told him to call me if he ever needed an aerospace consultancy. Then my memory fast-forwards to the night we broke up, before we even left for the observatory. *"If you have a billionaire friend with a kink for outer space, please send them my way. I won't take your money, but I'll gladly take theirs."*

Guess a big movie studio qualifies as an entity moving around billions.

Coincidence? Could the out-of-the-blue offer and Christian be unrelated? No, two and two only ever add up to four. Hollywood has never knocked on our doors before. Christian has to be the one behind this unusual request.

But why?

Why now?

We broke up over a month ago, and I haven't heard a peep from him since the night of the crash. I'm barely starting to function as a proper human being again after the second disastrous— and, this time, really heart-shattering—breakup this year.

Why sneak back into my life now? Are he and Olivia Thornton over? There haven't been new pictures of them in the papers for at least a week. Is that why he's reaching out?

"Err, Lana?" Dr. Conway's voice brings me back to his office.

"Yes?" I blush under the scrutiny of my adviser.

"So, are you willing to consult for the studio?" he asks.

"Um." I feel like a trapped animal. "Can't somebody else from the department do it?"

"The studio has specifically requested you," Dr. Conway says, X-raying me with a penetrating stare that tells me my boss reads gossip magazines.

"How much time did they give us to accept or refuse?"

"A week."

A week, that's good. I don't have to decide right now. "Then maybe could I possibly wait to see if Piloto comes forward with an offer?"

My adviser sighs. "Lana, I can't tell you what to do. If you've been in talks with Piloto, I'm sure they'll extend you an offer. But why wait? The offer from Denouement Studios is real and more than generous. It would cover not only your grant but also that of the other student who lost her funding when StaxiaVix went bankrupt."

"And she hasn't found another sponsor yet?"

Dr. Conway shakes his head. "Her project was more targeted toward StaxiaVix's core business. It's a niche. She's having a hard time finding someone else interested in sponsoring her research."

I've lost. Even if I were willing to gamble my future on a different offer coming in, I could never leave a fellow woman in STEM to hang out to dry. Already there are so few of us; we need to support each other.

"You can tell Denouement Studios I accept their offer." I nod in defeat. "Did they give you a schedule?"

"Filming starts in one week. We will work out a schedule with them around your lectures and office hours. Someone from the studios will email you once everything is settled. And cheer up," my adviser concludes. "This is good news."

With a lump in my throat, I attempt a smile and get up, saying, "Of course."

On trembling legs, I walk out of the office and rush to the library to get Marjory's opinion on this unexpected development. I even forget poor Trevor and all the data I left him to collect.

31

CHRISTIAN

The day after we start filming *The Descendant of Dawn*, I'm in my trailer busy memorizing my lines when the walkie-talkie on the foldable table near the door crackles to life.

"Boss." Penny's voice comes all snappy and distorted from the other side. "Are you there?"

I pick up the small radio. "Present and listening, over."

"I've to signal a very angry rocket scientist marching your way. She'll be at your door in three, two—"

Penny's voice is drowned out by the pounding of fists on the trailer's door.

I turn off the radio, get up, and compose my features in an easygoing expression before opening the door.

Even if Penny forewarned me, nothing could've prepared me for the turmoil that spreads through my gut at seeing Lana for the first time in over a month.

"Hi," I say, hoping to read the same emotions on her inscrutable face. Wearing her hair down, a flowy black skirt, and a simple "There's no planet B" T-shirt... man, she's beautiful.

"Hi," she says back. And where her features were set on anger before, she seems uncertain now.

So I smile. "It's good to see you." Again, she looks taken aback by my friendliness. "You want to come in?"

Lana nods and climbs the few steps into the trailer. As we come face to face, I have to muster all my self-control not to close the door behind her and crush her against it in a passionate kiss. I'm dying to hug her, to drop to one knee and beg her to take me back, but I know I have to play it cool for now. Assess where we stand first.

Still, I can't help but say, "You look good."

Sapphire eyes widen in surprise. She opens her mouth to say something but then changes her mind.

She's flustered.

Good. Flustered, I can work with. It's indifference that would've put a nail in my heart's coffin.

"Why?" she says.

I don't need to ask what the question is referring to. She wants to know why I've dragged her back into my life.

"You said to call you if I ever needed a space consultancy. Turns out I did."

"That was before..."

"You broke up with me?" I finish for her. Better remind her who dumped who, and why, before I try to explain Olivia. "I thought we could still be friends."

"Friends?" She spits out the word as if it's acid.

Even better. I don't want to be her friend.

"Yeah, why not? The opportunity came up, the studios needed a scientific consultancy on the script. They have big pockets and this is a big-budget movie. I thought I'd kill two birds with one stone and have them fund your research. And I'm sure your technical insight will make the script a million times better." I don't tell her I've had a few scientific mistakes inserted on purpose for her to catch.

"The donation was very generous," Lana concedes. I can tell she's fighting to keep an even tone. "Do all script consultancies pay that well?"

"This is Hollywood, everything is overpriced. And I have some pull with the producers."

"I'm sure you do."

I can't tell if she's happy or peeved.

She crosses her arms over her chest and gives me a curt, "Well, thank you, I guess."

"You're welcome. Want to meet the woman who made it all possible?"

A buffer will help us stay civil; we've been alone enough for a first reunion. I can tell my being so casual about everything is infuriating her, and whatever explosive mix is boiling inside Lana's head, I'd prefer not to face it alone.

"Sure," she says briskly, and precedes me out of the trailer.

32

LANA

Friends.

Ah!

I count to ten, but counting to a hundred wouldn't help me calm down right now. As I follow Christian around the set, I'm simmering with suppressed rage.

Oh, so now he wants us to be friends.

First, he makes me fall for him without telling me who he really is. Then, he drags me into his crazy life. And when I panic for a second, he forgets about me in a few hours and starts dating a supermodel turned actress the next morning.

But now Christian remembers I exist, and he wants to be flipping, frigging *friends*. And I can't even hate him for convincing the studios to hire me because with his gesture he's helping at least one woman in STEM who wouldn't have been able to complete her Ph.D. otherwise. I'm talking about the other student. I still believe Piloto would've come through for me in the end.

Still, how long will I be able to withstand this torture? To be near him without being able to touch, kiss, or even hug him. To be the friendly ex while the new, famous girlfriend visits him on set.

I swear that if I see Olivia here, I won't be responsible for my actions.

As we walk across the stages, I'm so lost in my own thoughts that when Christian stops walking, I almost bump into him, face to back. But thank goodness I'm able to stop with an inch to spare.

Christian waves to attract the attention of a tall, sleek blonde who's busy talking into a headset. The woman, dressed in a black pencil skirt suit, high stiletto heels, and with a straight, shoulder-length bob without a hair out of place, looks like she means business.

When she spots Christian, she taps the mic once. "I have to go now, Pier, but keep me informed on any new developments." Then, with a big smile, she walks toward us. "Christian."

"Samantha, allow me to introduce you to Lana."

"Ah." Her brown eyes turn to me with keen interest, only to flick back to Christian and back to me again. *What's with the look?* "What a pleasure to finally meet you," she says. "Christian has told me amazing things about you. We're thrilled to have you on board."

Did he now?

I throw him an uncertain stare, then turn to Samantha. "Thank you for sponsoring my research."

Samantha waves me off. "Oh, please, the publicity alone will repay the investment. The movie studio producing a space flick while sponsoring real-life research on space rockets, it's—" She stops abruptly and presses her hand to her left ear. "Yes?" she says into the mic. "Yes, he's here, I'll send him your way." Then, looking up at Christian, she adds, "You're needed at hair and makeup. You can leave Lana with me; I'll show her around."

With half a grin and a mock bow, Christian says, "Ladies," and goes on his way.

And if it upset me to see him again, watching him go is ten times worse.

To preserve a shred of mental health, I hope my involvement with this production will be a short affair. I haven't even understood what they want me to do yet.

"Lana, welcome once again to the team. Let me give you the tour." Samantha links her arm with mine and guides me toward a squat, rectangular building with no windows. "Unfortunately, there's not much to see here, as we're mostly shooting our VFX scenes in LA."

"Oh, where's the rest of the production?"

"Vancouver," she says, effectively plunging a knife into my heart.

Christian will be gone soon. We'll be even farther apart.

"But don't worry," Samantha continues. "We won't ask you to follow us there. You should be able to complete your revisions while we're still here."

"And what is it exactly I'm doing?"

Samantha pulls the heavy-looking metal door to the building open and shows me inside. "To start, we'd like you to review the script and tell us what you think."

We enter a dark room, which looks like the command deck of a spaceship surrounded by acid-green walls.

"Isn't it too late to change the story if you've already started filming?" I ask.

"We're still transitioning from the pre-production phase, really; certain things had to be *rushed...*" she says with the tone of someone who hates rushing things and had her hand forced on the matter. "And we're not asking for a developmental edit, anyway. Just a final technical pass to make sure all the scientific details are in order."

"Am I searching for something in particular?"

238 CAMILLA ISLEY

"Anything that stands out as weird or scientifically inaccurate."

"Aren't spaceships inaccurate per se?" I ask. "Is the movie set in a hypothetical future? How can I tell what futuristic technology is plausible and what's not?"

"Devil's in the details." Samantha's smile falters; guess she isn't used to getting the third degree from her employees. She looks like a woman who asks questions as opposed to answering them. "The story takes place in a fantasy universe, but, for example, we kept the military ranking consistent with the US armed forces and hired an expert to check there weren't any inconsistencies. The same goes for you: we just want to make sure we aren't breaking too many laws of physics. Like having a ship make a big boom when it explodes in space."

That she knows the vacuum of space wouldn't carry sounds surprises me. Finally, a language I understand.

"Makes sense," I say. "So, what's the movie about?"

"An evil villain tries to conquer the galaxy and a redemption story arc where our renegade hero pilot saves the world. While falling in love, of course."

My throat fills with acid greener than the walls. Will I have to witness Christian getting all smoochy on set with another impossibly beautiful actress while I'm here?

Samantha points at the stage. "This is the main ship's command deck, where—" Again, she stops speaking mid-sentence to press a hand to her ear. "Come again... No... Yes... No, *don't...* I'll be right there." Then to me, "Sorry, Lana, I have to cut the tour short." She ushers me back out of the building. "We weren't able to provide you with a dedicated trailer, but Christian said you can use his to work if that's okay with you?"

And I hate myself because the first thing that pops into my head is: *is there a bed in the trailer?*

Then I sober up and ask, "If I have to read the script, can't I do it from home?"

At my question, fear flashes behind Samantha's eyes, a reaction that makes little sense. "No, sorry."

A lie, I can't help thinking. But why? Why would she want to keep me here at all costs?

So I ask her, "Why not?"

"We... err..." Then her expression changes from worried and uncertain back to her confident, down-to-business smile. "The script is still confidential, of course. We couldn't risk having it leaked." Then, putting a hand forward, she continues. "And I'm not saying you're not trustworthy, it's... mmm... the studio's policy to have no copies leave the premises."

I feel like she just fed me a load of bullshit.

But... job security, Lana; just do as the business lady in the nice suit tells you.

"I understand," I say.

"Do you remember how to get to Christian's trailer?"

"I'm sure I can manage."

"Very well." Samantha gives my arm a gentle squeeze. "I'll have someone bring you a copy of the script."

By the time I find my way back to Christian's trailer, Penelope is already there waiting for me with a stack of papers in her hands. And it's honestly good to see her again. I missed her dry sarcasm and bubbly personality.

"Lana." She pulls me into a hug. "Long time no see. It's great to have you back. How have you been?"

Miserable, I want to say. But I go for a shrug and a chiller, "Fine. Busy with work. You?"

"Been weaving a shroud I'm happy to finally unweave."

After that mysterious and slightly mythological statement, she unlocks the door, gives me a copy of the script, and leaves me alone.

Inside, I give the trailer a quick once-over. No bed, but there's a couch that could host two people comfortably if they were lying one on top of the other while—

Whoa.

Let's not go there.

Nothing is going to happen here, no matter what fantasies my dirty mind comes up with. *Christian wants to be friends.* The worst offense possible in the ex-boyfriend book. I'd prefer it if he felt a raging hate toward me, a feeling strong enough to mirror the passion I thought we shared. But what's friendship? It's like saying, I like you and respect you as a person, but I have for you the same desire I feel toward an expired yogurt cup.

I sit at the small, foldable table and stare at the bundle of papers in my hands:

The Descendant of Dawn
Screenplay by Adrian J. Moore

Okay, Mr. Moore, let's see how much of a science moron you are. And if I hurry, I can be out of this trailer before Christian comes back and never have to see him again.

33

CHRISTIAN

"Did you have to keep me on set so long?" I complain to Samantha, walking out of the green-wall room. "Lana has left already."

One head shake from Penny warned me of Lana's departure as soon as we finished shooting.

"Not my fault," Samantha says. "That woman is a machine."

I walk to my trailer while Samantha and a costume designer follow me. "So, how did it go with the screenplay?"

"Lana found all the mistakes we planted, plus a few more that we didn't. Really, I should thank you for bringing her on board, regardless of your personal agenda."

At my very specific request for a certain female consultant to join the team, Samantha became suspicious, so I had to fess up and tell her the truth.

"So, what's Lana's next assignment?" I ask. And to get rid of the costume designer, I take off the leather jacket I'm wearing and hand it to her. Precious jacket secured, the young woman leaves me and Samantha alone in front of my trailer.

"Chris, that woman isn't stupid," Samantha protests. "Already today she caught me lying to keep her here as long as I could. Also, don't you think it's wrong to waste her time on bogus assignments?"

"Yeah, it's wrong. But I'm a desperate man, Sam. And if my plan to reconnect with her works, she won't think of it as wasted time."

"What if she wants nothing to do with you?"

"Then I'll accept it, and she'll still get the grant from the studios. She'll leave better off anyway; I'm the only one who stands to lose."

Samantha crosses her arms, tapping her shoe on the concrete. She has her actors-being-difficult pout on. "I don't know what else to—"

I open the door of my trailer and turn to interrupt Samantha. "I don't care what you have to do. If you have to ask her for a list of good buzzwords to make the movie sound more science-y. Or if you have to ask her to write fake equations for space travel. Have her build a fake rocket from scratch. Whatever it takes, I want Lana here every day. I gave up on her once, I won't do it again."

"Calm down, stallion," Samantha says. "I'll see what I can do. But whatever big, romantic gesture you're planning, I suggest you get on with it."

"You make sure Lana keeps coming on set, and I'll take care of the romance."

34

LANA

Seeing Christian, having access to him again, becomes a drug. I know he's no good for me, but I can't stay away. I need my daily fix. When I arrive on set each day, my eyes immediately scan the room to find him. When I'm working in his trailer, my ears strain for the telling sounds of him approaching—*like I'm doing right now.* And when he's nowhere to be found, all my mind can think about is him.

It's like the universe is conspiring to prevent my heart from healing. I've tried to get away from this production, but the more quickly and efficiently I solve any problem they throw my way, the more absurd the next task becomes.

And the worst part is that being around Christian is almost too easy. We've fallen back into a sort of intimacy. We talk, we share jokes, and if I wasn't the wiser, I'd say we flirt—with words, stares, and the occasional unintentional touch that sets my skin on fire.

It drives me crazy every time it happens, especially because I can never tell if Christian made contact by mistake or accidentally on purpose.

The only mercy I've had is that Olivia Thornton hasn't

appeared on set. Neither have more pictures of her and Christian surfaced in the news. And I don't subscribe to any gossip magazine, but scanning their covers whenever I pass a display has become a small obsession. Same as my new mania of marking the passing of time.

I've circled on the calendar the days until the crew moves to Vancouver. And if I couldn't wait for the time to fly by at the beginning of shooting, the more squares I cross off, the more an irrational fear mounts in my guts. No matter that having this extra job on top of my research, on top of my teaching, on top of my volunteering has me falling into bed exhausted every night. I've never felt more alive.

What will I do when he's out of my life for good? A whole country away? What then?

I honestly can't say what the worse torture could be: to spend time with Christian in a look-but-don't-touch way, or to not see him at all.

Guess I'll find out soon enough.

"Lana!" The small radio sitting on the foldable table in Christian's trailer comes alive, startling me.

I grab it, fumbling with a few buttons before I find the right one, and press it. "Yeah."

"You're needed at stage four," Samantha's distorted voice informs me.

"I'll be right there," I say, settling the radio back on its charger column.

I exit the trailer with a sigh. *What now?*

* * *

When I enter the building that contains stage four, I wonder for a second if I went to the wrong set by mistake. The place is dark and empty. But when I peek back out the door, a plaque on the wall reading "Stage 4" confirms I'm in the right place.

Inside, the almost absolute darkness is broken only by the flickering light coming from a projector hanging from the ceiling.

"Hello?" I call.

In response, a white fabric screen lowers from above, turning the light from the projector into a galaxy. My eyes follow the star system as it moves on the screen until it settles on a particular constellation.

And I've spent enough nights staring at this particular slice of the sky to immediately recognize the Christiana sitting in its center.

"What...?" I ask the darkness.

"Hey," a familiar voice calls from behind me.

I turn to find Christian walking toward me still wearing his pilot costume—dusty, worn-out jeans, leather jacket, and messy hair.

Not fair, he's practically irresistible like that.

"What is this?" I ask.

"A romantic setting." He stops a few feet away and looks at the fake sky. "What do you think?"

"Is this a joke? Because it isn't funny."

"No joke," Christian says, coming a step closer. "You like it?"

"I'm not sure your girlfriend would approve."

Or maybe she's one of those confident women who doesn't worry about exes.

"My—" He frowns slightly in confusion. "You mean Olivia?"

"Yeah, whatever her name is."

"You sound jealous."

"Am not."

Christian's lips curve in a warm smile.

What the hell does he have to smile about?

"Because if you were jealous," Christian says, "you'd have no reason to be."

A slow burning starts in my belly and my throat goes dry. "Why not?"

"The relationship with Olivia was fake."

What the hell is he talking about?

"What do you mean, *fake?*"

"A business arrangement." He takes another step toward me. "You said you wanted the press off your back, so I fed them a different story to obsess over."

"You what?" My knees threaten to give way. "None of it was real?"

"No."

"But the pictures...?"

"All staged for the benefit of the paparazzi."

I sway under the weight of this new information, but Christian is there to catch me.

I look up at him. "But I believed it."

"I'm so sorry," Christian says sincerely.

"I wanted to call you the next day, tell you I'd made a mistake, but then I saw the pictures..."

An expression of genuine regret crosses his face. "I've been an idiot."

I want to hit him, but I can't because he's holding my wrists to his chest. So I lash out with words. "You tortured me for weeks."

"I'm sorry," he repeats.

"Why tell me now?" I push back to get away from him, but he doesn't let me go. "I've been here for days; why wait?"

"I wanted to remind you first."

"Remind me of what?"

"That you laugh at my jokes, that you like to flirt with me, that your skin burns at my touch..."

So it was all on purpose. "Is that why you made the studios hire me?"

"Yes."

"Why?"

His gaze is unfaltering as he says, "Because I'm in love with you."

BOOM!

This time a whole Big Bang is happening in my belly.

I close my eyes and a single tear slides down my cheek. *Is this real?* I don't trust my senses.

I blink a few times, then ask, "You never said it before...?"

"'Cause I'm an even bigger idiot."

My heart breaks and heals at the same time.

"You love me?"

"I do."

I look at him, still not able to believe what he's saying. The doubt must show in my eyes because Christian says, "I love you, Lana, so much that if you suffered from short-term amnesia and forgot me every night as you went to sleep, I'd make you fall in love with me all over again the next day."

What?

"I don't have amnesia," I say.

"Okay, then, I love you so much that I'd run after you in the snow wearing only tiny knickers."

"It never snows in LA."

"Doesn't matter, I'd do it anyway. And if we were ever on a sinking boat in the middle of a freezing ocean, you could have my wooden plank."

"Nothing of what you just said makes sense," I say, smiling and crying a little at the same time. "But I'll take it."

"How about this?" He cups my face with one hand. "I love you, all the way to the stars and back." Christian points at the glittering sky surrounding us.

It doesn't matter what he's saying, what he can or cannot put into words because it's all in his eyes.

Love Theorem.

Hypothesis: he's looking at me like I'm the sun and the moon and the stars in the sky and the love of his life.

Conclusion: He really is in love with me.

"And I know nothing has changed," Christian continues, oblivious to the marvelous realization that has just taken place in my brain. "That my life is probably still too much for you—"

"Shhhh." I press a finger to his lips. "The day after we broke up, I also wanted to tell you I don't care about any of that. That all I want is to be with you."

I lower my hand from his mouth, and let him ask, "You don't care anymore?"

"No."

"Are you sure?"

"Yes."

"How can you be?"

"Because this past month without you has been the worst of my life. Because leaving you broke my heart and gave me palpitations. Because every night, even when I thought you were dating someone else, I spent hours staring at our star." Christian's face lights up at my words, so I give him the last missing piece. "And because I love you, too," I say. "To the stars and back."

EPILOGUE

CHRISTIAN

Three Years Later

"And the Oscar goes to..." Julia Roberts pauses to open the envelope. "...Christian Slade, *The Man by the Sea.*"

I don't trust my hearing at first, but Lana's little hand squeeze confirms that it's really happening.

Best actor. I won the Oscar.

Head spinning, I turn to stare at my wife, and the smile she gives me is worth a thousand golden statuettes.

I kiss her and then stand up.

The short walk to the stage seems to last forever and makes me glad I'm not a woman in heels. Now I get Lana's fussing and fear of falling whenever she has to wear heels—like tonight.

I hop up one, two, three, four, five, six, seven steps, and then I'm on the main stage walking toward its center.

Julia, looking resplendent in a shiny black gown, hands me the statuette. As my fingers close around the cold metal, I feel like the luckiest man on earth—although, tragically, no longer the sexiest. I haven't won the title for two years now, snatched away from me by the new guy on the block: Diego O'Donnell, just as Samantha had predicted.

Also, as an older—in Hollywood years—happily married man in real life, I'm no longer directors' number one choice to play the romantic hero. So my life, alongside my career, is finally moving in the direction I've always wanted it to go. And all thanks to the love of one extraordinary woman.

I grab the mic and clear my throat before launching into my acceptance speech.

"Thank you to the Academy, to my director, producers, and fellow cast members. Thank you to my wife." I pause to point at Lana. "Not only for making my life special every day but also for picking this screenplay out of the stack for me."

Lana watches movies now, but I swear she still prefers reading the screenplays to seeing the stories on screen. She devours all the scripts I receive, even those that Penny discards, and she's become my number-one adviser on what movies to make.

"We're both very passionate about the environment," I continue my address to the theater. "So this movie had a special meaning for both of us. And as better actors have said before me" —I nod at Leo, sitting in the first row—"climate change is real, and it's happening right now!"

I pause again to let the applause die down.

"*The Man by the Sea* is a dystopian movie about life on a wasted planet Earth, but while we were filming, our entire crew couldn't help but wonder how much of what we were portraying was fiction and how much was prophesy. My wife and I, we're helping to shape the leaders of tomorrow, fostering a better education system so they will lead humanity on the right path one day. But while we wait for future generations to do a better job than us, we have to take responsibility for today. It's a minute to midnight. The clock is ticking, and if we want our children to see the dawn of another bright day on our beautiful planet, we need to take action now."

Wow, I might've gotten a little carried away. I can already imagine Penny teasing me, saying I've finally earned my Greenpeace cap. But it's all worth it because Lana is smiling at me so widely, with such overwhelming pride, that it feels like a balloon is threatening to burst in my chest.

"Thank you," I conclude.

I lift the Oscar to the sky, then lower the statuette to kiss its head and point it at Lana, mouthing, "I love you."

$$* * *$$

Lana

I listen to Christian's acceptance speech with tears shining in my eyes. He's worked so hard to win an Oscar, and I'm so proud of him and the message he's sending to the world.

A lot has changed from those first rocky months of our relationship. Now that we're a married couple and old news to the press, the paparazzi aren't so keen on following us everywhere we go. Even if tailing us—with Christian's reduced car fleet—would be much easier.

I've convinced my husband to auction off eighteen of his twenty cars and donate the proceeds to different WWF projects—reforestation, the cleaning of the oceans, and wildlife preservation. Now we only have two cars, a Tesla and a Ferrari—*the hybrid model.*

Fewer cars are not the only change I've brought into Christian's life. Since I moved in with him, our home is less white and a lot messier. We've also made it a self-sustaining house powered entirely by solar panels.

Cengel and Boles love living in a mansion and having a private chef. They almost completely refuse cat food now and only eat our scraps.

Chef Jeff is still teaching us to cook, and I've also asked him to host a few elective classes in our charter schools. We've instituted a yearly scholarship that we award to a student Jeff has hand-picked to go to culinary school.

Hey, we can't all be rocket scientists.

As for me, I completed my research on hybrid rocket propulsion and earned my Doctor of Philosophy degree at UCLA. But I left academia behind and applied my new shiny title to the best of causes: provide free education to as many young minds as we can. My full-time job now is to lead Christian's foundation, Teachers Without Postcodes. There's so much more I can do from this position, so many more kids I can bring better education to while still following my passion for teaching. My first act was to institute a summer space camp, where young students can learn everything from how pee is recycled in space to how rocket propulsion works. And more and more of our high school graduates are enrolling in STEM degrees as they progress to college—many with a fully-funded scholarship, many also women.

The new role also gives me the flexibility to teach science classes when we're here in LA, but to follow Christian to whatever filming location he's headed to around the world.

We're happy, and there's only one thing missing in our lives right now.

I gently caress my belly.

We started trying for a baby a month ago, and from his words, I can tell Christian is as eager as I am to grow our family. And this speech—*wow!* He didn't write one, said it'd be bad luck, so he's talking off the cuff and really hammering down on the environmental cause.

"...we need to take action now. Thank you," Christian finishes, and the room explodes with applause.

I join in and clap until my palms hurt, beaming at my husband as he kisses the Oscar and then points it at me, mouthing, "I love you."

And only he can read the answer on my lips, "To the stars and back."

AUTHOR'S NOTE

Dear Reader,

I hope you enjoyed reading *The Love Theorem* as much as I enjoyed writing it and giving it a fabulous makeover worthy of a nineties rom-com with the help of my amazing publisher Boldwood Books.

If you loved this story, we're happy to bring you three more books to binge read in this series.

Are you looking for an adventure? Book two follows Lana's best friend, Winter, on an exhilarating photography expedition in beautiful Thailand. This story features a treasure hunt, funny exploits, and, of course, a gorgeous, brooding archaeologist who drives Winter crazy in the best enemies-to-lovers, grumpy-sunshine rom-com fashion. In this book, you'll also meet Archibald Hill, a tall, blond, bearded supporting character with piercing blue eyes and a devil-may-care personality who stole my heart and snatched his own love story in book three of the series. Turn the page for a sneak peek at Winter's story.

As for book four, Samantha Baker is the protagonist. You might've noticed Christian's favorite producer is a bit of a posh city girl and hates being away from New York. So, of course, evil little me, I'm going to send her to the country to supervise the off-track production of Christian's latest small-town rom-com. And who knows if a local cowboy will make her reconsider the hardships of not having a Starbucks within twenty miles. A sweet, enemies to lovers rom-com.

Now, I have to ask you a big favor. If you loved my story, please consider leaving a review on your favorite retailer's website, on Goodreads, or wherever you like to post reviews (your blog, Book-Tok, in a text to your best friend...) Reviews are the best gift you can give to an author, and word of mouth is the most powerful means of book discovery.

Thank you for your constant support!

Camilla, x

MORE FROM CAMILLA ISLEY

We hope you enjoyed reading *The Love Theorem*. If you did, please leave a review.

If you'd like to gift a copy, this book is also available as an ebook, hardback, large print, digital audio download and audiobook CD.

Sign up to Camilla Isley's mailing list for news, competitions and updates on future books.

https://bit.ly/CamillaIsleyNews

Discover more fun-filled romantic comedies from Camilla Isley...

ABOUT THE AUTHOR

Camilla Isley is an engineer who left science behind to write bestselling contemporary rom-coms set all around the world. She lives in Italy.

Visit Camilla's website: https://camillaisley.com

Follow Camilla Isley on social media:

instagram.com/camillaisley

tiktok.com/@camilla.isley

facebook.com/camillaisley

twitter.com/camillaisley

bookbub.com/authors/camilla-isley

youtube.com/RomanceAudiobooks

Boldwood

Boldwood Books is an award-winning fiction publishing company seeking out the best stories from around the world.

Find out more at www.boldwoodbooks.com

Join our reader community for brilliant books, competitions and offers!

Follow us
@BoldwoodBooks
@BookandTonic

Sign up to our weekly deals newsletter

https://bit.ly/BoldwoodBNewsletter

Printed in Great Britain
by Amazon

24581844R00149